Money for Millennials

How to Celebrate Financial Freedom by 30

Isabella Hong

Putting Words
publishing

A catalogue record for this book is available from the
National Library of Australia.

ISBN: 978-0-6456666-8-7 (Paperback)
978-0-6456666-2-5 (E-book)

Produced by **Putting Words**
Cover Design by Ashish Joshi
Putting Words
PO Box 5062
Wonga Park,
Victoria, Australia. 3115
www.puttingwords.com
books@puttingwords.com

Dedication

This book is dedicated to the fearless women
chasing their aspirations and dreams.
May you triumph over any hindrances
and release the limitless power within you.
Dream without limits and financial success
will be within your grasp.

Disclaimer

This book provides general information only and is not intended to provide financial, legal, or tax advice. The information in the book may not be up-to-date, accurate, or complete, and relying on it is strictly at the reader's own risk. The author and publisher are not responsible for any loss or damage, including loss of profits, that may arise from the use or reliance on the information in the book. Readers should consult a financial consultant before making any financial decisions and understand that the book is for informational purposes only and not a substitute for professional advice. By reading the book, the reader agrees to the terms and conditions outlined in the disclaimer.

Contents

Foreword

I first became interested in achieving Financial Freedom at the age of 25. I wish I had started earlier, but as the saying goes, the best time to start was ten years ago, and the next best time is now. And for the readers here, I am glad you are picking up this book now.

I am pleased to write the Foreword for *Money for Millennials: How to Celebrate Financial Freedom by 30*. I first had the privilege of meeting Isabella Hong a couple of years ago, and I have seen firsthand her unwavering commitment to empowering people to take control of their financial future. Her branding tag, Financial Missy, truly reflects her strong persona, and this book is a testament to her passion and dedication to financial freedom.

When I first started on my journey to search for financial freedom at the age of 25, I wish I had a guide like this. It could have saved me from losing nearly $100k in investing and wasting a lot of time. Isabella's story is both inspiring and relatable, and she shares practical strategies and actionable steps that are relevant for any millennial seeking financial independence.

This book is not just about financial strategies or portfolio optimisation; it's about overcoming limiting beliefs and breaking free from financial entitlement. Isabella's voice is bold and unmatched and speaks directly to the heart of her readers, urging them to act and make a real difference in their lives.

The 50/15/10/5 rule and the Earn, Protect, Save, and Invest Framework are just two of the many tools she shares with her readers, making it easier for them to create a continuous cycle of passive income and wealth accumulation. The insights and tips in this book are valuable and relevant for any millennial seeking to celebrate financial freedom.

Now is the time to free yourself from the shackles of financial insecurity and start celebrating life the way you should! I highly recommend this book to anyone who wants to achieve financial freedom. Thank you, Isabella, for sharing your story and empowering us with your insights and expertise.

Isabella Hong, also known as Financial Missy, is a true inspiration, and this book is a must-read for anyone who wants to achieve financial freedom.

Sean Seah,
Author, *Financial Joy*

Preface

As I reflect on my childhood, I realise how privileged I was to grow up in a family that didn't have to worry about finances. My parents worked hard to provide for us, and I'm grateful for my comfortable life. However, this privilege also comes with a downside. The value of money was not a common topic discussed, so I didn't grow up appreciating its worth.

I was one of those annoying self-entitled millennials I now hate. As a result of growing up with a domestic helper who took excellent care of me while my parents worked, things only got awry. I lived like a princess at home because she would serve me, and I never had to do a thing. It is embarrassing to admit that before I became a student nurse, I never knew how to make a cup of Milo or make my bed.

Looking back, I now realise I took my comfortable lifestyle for granted. I remember vividly the times I would throw tantrums whenever I didn't get what I wanted. I didn't realise the amount of work and sacrifice it took to earn the money that paid for my upbringing. It wasn't until I became a nurse that I realised the importance of managing money and making sound financial decisions.

I achieved a mediocre score during my GCE A levels, which seemed to limit my academic options, but it turned out to be such a blessing in disguise in hindsight. I had picked nursing as the only surefire course I knew I had a good shot at getting into. Surprisingly, I survived and enjoyed nursing school. During my six years as a registered nurse, I learned the importance of financial health to overall well-being as I cared for people from all walks of life. I witnessed patients struggling to make ends meet and others who could focus on their health and recovery without worrying about the cost of care.

It pained me to witness how the underprivileged struggle with their lives. One particular home visit during my nursing career still sticks with me. The house was poorly lit and reeked of bodily fluids. The one-room rental flat was infested with cockroaches, ants, and bed bugs, even on my patient. While I tip-toed around the house, praying that I wouldn't bring any home, he would nonchalantly slap them dead with his bare hands. It was a sobering wake-up call for me, witnessing firsthand how poverty affects one's life and health.

There is a vicious cycle of poverty, and I knew I could make a difference. The fact that I began investing when I was 19 gave me a headstart over many others in breaking free from the rat race. I believe I can have a meaningful impact on the people around me and the larger community. I can help by teaching people how to make smart financial decisions and let money work hard for them so they can enjoy their retirement free from financial worry.

At 30, I achieved financial freedom and now live life on my terms. I left my stable nursing career to explore entrepreneurship in the finance industry. Only then did I realise how intimidated people feel about money. Those who did not understand it saw it as a complicated, mysterious subject that experts could only explain. It didn't have to be this way!

My goal in writing this book is to break down the complexities of finance and make it more approachable for everyone. I firmly believe that financial freedom is achievable for anyone, regardless of their background or level of experience. Through my own journey of overcoming 19 years of entitlement and limiting beliefs, I achieved financial freedom by age 30. I am confident that you can too! It's never too late to start somewhere. Whether you're just starting out as an undergraduate or you're a seasoned life warrior, the principles and strategies outlined in this book can help you make informed financial decisions and reach your goals.

How Should You Read This Book?

I have written this book in a narrative format to reflect my natural thought process of self-awareness, budgeting, and the strategies that I personally used to achieve financial freedom. My goal in using this format is to engage readers in a relatable way. I want to demonstrate that financial success is attainable for anyone willing to put in the effort and make informed decisions.

To maximise the benefits of this book, it is highly recommended that you read it in order. This is because the chapters are arranged in a logical progression of information and ideas. Chapters 1-3 focus on reinforcing your mindset, while Chapters 4 and 5 delve into the fundamentals of money management. Finally, Chapters 6-10 provide a detailed breakdown of my strategies to optimise my personal finance portfolio. In Chapter 11, I provide a practical guide to help you bring everything together and create a personalised financial plan tailored to your goals and circumstances.

It is important to note that everyone's financial situation is unique, and what worked for me may not work for you. While drawing on my diverse background as a nurse, financial consultant, and investor, I offer insights gained from working with a wide range of clients. I aim to inspire and empower readers to take control of their financial futures by sharing my personal experiences. With this in mind, it is essential to consider your own circumstances and make informed decisions based on your individual needs and goals. I hope that my experiences and insights can provide valuable guidance and support as you work towards achieving your version of financial freedom.

By the end of this book, I want you to feel confident and equipped to make informed and strategic decisions about your finances. Whether you're just starting out on your financial journey or looking to take your wealth-building efforts to the next level, the insights and strategies in this book can help you get there. I want you to feel confident and empowered to make thoughtful decisions about your money. This is true whether you want to build wealth, save for retirement, or manage your budget more effectively.

I hope this book will inspire you to take control of your financial future and provide a clear roadmap for achieving your financial goals. With the insights and strategies provided, I believe that you can achieve financial freedom and take charge of your financial well-being.

CHAPTER 1

Inventing Reality

Your experiences shape your reality, but they're only a tiny piece of the puzzle. To see the bigger picture, keep an open mind and learn from other perspectives too.

In my business as a thought leader in finance, I always enjoy posing this question to all my clients at our first meeting. "What is your financial goal?"

A seemingly innocent question is almost invariably met with the response, "F.I.R.E., duh."

Who doesn't want to achieve Financial Independence and Retire Early? Imagine yourself sipping a Mai Tai by a beach in Bali today. Then, explore ancient Incan ruins in Peru next week. Then shop for luxury goods in France the week after. How exhilarating, being able to do whatever you want without worrying about anything. From what I said in my Preface, my personal goal is pretty much the same – to retire by 40 and contribute my time to humanitarian organisations.

And to do that, we need sufficient savings to safeguard our own future, don't we?

However, for those of us born without a silver spoon to achieve the above, we would need to slave away at our jobs and make huge personal sacrifices along the way. "Hard work is a virtue", you murmur under your breath, remembering the endless drills at school and your parents' exhortations to always do more, always be better. You work hard, but promotions and pay raises never seem to be within your grasp because you're at the bottom of the corporate hierarchy. You grit your teeth and just push through because no pain, no gain, right?

Even when you're sick, you're expected to keep an eye on your work chats to ensure that work is on track and you're always available, just in case. There's no work-life balance, but you can't quit until you find a job that pays more and everyone tells you it's a terrible idea to leave a job without a concrete backup plan.

At the end of it, you've finally amassed enough wealth to indulge in what you want – but what do you want? You've alienated yourself from your friends by running the rat race relentlessly. Who will you hang out with? You've become a virtual stranger to your family. Who will you travel with? You've had no time to discover or indulge in any hobbies. What will you do with all that spare time?

Was it worth it? Is this the life that you've always wanted? But that's reality, you might argue. Is it really? Do you really need to hold down a boring job, hating what you do but feeling stuck? Do you really need to work hard in the traditional sense? What is reality?

Here, dear reader, I'd like to introduce you to the idea that reality as you know it is not fixed but is your own personal experience that is influenced by various forces – society, mass media, culture, politics, etc. Through understanding, analysing, and controlling how you view *reality*, you can improve your lived experience. And that is why I enjoy asking my clients, "What is your financial goal?" to start understanding what my clients' perspectives and thought processes are like and to start helping them achieve the paradigm shifts necessary to help kick-start their journey toward wealth.

The Augmented Psychology Of Reality

Reality is that our perspectives are constantly influenced by our surroundings, which often strongly emphasise the importance of attaining financial security and stability. This emphasis on financial independence makes people prioritise making money over other aspects of life, such as pursuing passions and exploring creative outlets. It can leave people feeling stuck and with few options to change their current situation.

Growing up, my generation had a common saying that said, "Stay hard, get a good job, and you will be set for life." That's why we grew up with a strong emphasis on our finances, as we were taught that it was the key to living a happy and prosperous life. But the reality of today's world is that this is not always the case – many people are stuck in jobs they don't like, with no way to move forward!

It was inevitable that most young adults would reach a point of contention at some point in their lives. In what way does education determine future success? World-renowned individuals, such as Bill Gates, Steve Jobs, and Tony Robbins, have revolutionised their fields without formal education. *Is there a reason why I can't?*

With time, however, I have realised that education isn't just about acquiring knowledge but also about developing critical thinking skills, time management, and discipline. The fact remains that success can be achieved without a degree, but education can provide a strong foundation for achieving one's goals.

Coincidentally, my dad shared this story with me – his friend, Mr A., recently lamented that his son is considering dropping out of college because he believes it's a waste of time. A. Jr opened a food and beverage business a couple of years ago, but revenue has declined over the years, and during COVID-19, the business plummeted.

He borrowed a substantial sum from his aunt to set up the business and intended to borrow more to cover losses. In spite of the fact that he is about to graduate from college, A. Jr has no interest in pursuing a traditional university education. As he puts it, "Mark Zuckerberg didn't need a college degree to set up Facebook and succeed. There's no need to continue college." While I applaud A. Jr for not being afraid to fail, and he has the resilience to try, the numbers show otherwise.

The Taylor & Francis online study of 11,745 individuals in the US found that 94% of CEOs, judges, politicians, millionaires, billionaires, and business leaders attended college (Wai & Rindermann, 2017). The number of successful people without a college education appears to be in the minority, about six percent.

Sometimes we just believe what we want to believe. Still not convinced? Let's try it – close your eyes and picture yourself sucking on a lemon. What does it taste like?

Even as I write this, I am salivating already!

It's fascinating to learn how human psychology works. In the words of Tony Robbins, "Where focus goes, energy flows". If you are interested in Hermès bags, you will see many more people carrying them! Facebook analytics work just like this. The algorithm brings you similar results based on the content you have searched for.

In other words, what you feed your mind is a prediction of how your life will turn out. Therefore, it is essential to carefully consider what information you consume, as this will directly affect the outcomes you experience. There is nothing wrong with thinking that "Successful people are just lucky" simply because they were fortunate enough to be given the right opportunities in the right circumstances at the right moment. There is always truth in what you believe.

Luck plays a role in everything in life, big or small. If I'm lucky, I'll win the lottery – but to be lucky, I have to buy a ticket! For too long, we have heard that 90 percent of startups fail (Griffith, 2014). Skynova, a company specialising in online invoicing for small businesses, has estimated that it takes a startup three years on average to become profitable.

Entrepreneurship is not for the faint-hearted, and even seasoned entrepreneurs experience doubts and uncertainties from time to time. In fact, 36 percent of the entrepreneurs surveyed considered giving up at some point during their journey. But what sets those who succeed apart is their unwavering commitment to hard work, resilience, and sacrifice. To succeed, one must have grit, determination, and an unrelenting drive to persist despite challenges and setbacks.

Take the example of Tony Robbins, a self-made entrepreneur and motivational speaker who overcame homelessness and a challenging childhood to achieve extraordinary success. Robbins was once so down on his luck that he had to sleep on a friend's apartment floor or in homeless shelters. However, instead of giving up, he worked tirelessly to better himself, reading books, seeking guidance from mentors, and taking every opportunity to learn and grow. His relentless pursuit of personal development eventually led to him becoming one of our time's most influential motivational speakers. He inspired millions of people around the world to achieve their full potential.

Opportunities for success are everywhere, but they require more than just good luck. They demand a willingness to take risks, learn from failures, and keep pushing forward, no matter how tough the going gets. To succeed, you must be prepared to weather storms, embrace uncertainty, and firmly keep your eyes on your goals. And if you're willing to put in the arduous work, resilience, and sacrifice required, you, too, can achieve extraordinary success in whatever field you choose. The only question is: are you ready to take the first step towards realising your dreams?

New Measures of Success

Congratulations on earning your first academic degree! This is a significant achievement and marks the beginning of an exciting phase in your life. While you may no longer be expected to focus solely on getting good grades, you must also recognise that learning never stops. As an entrepreneur, I've come to appreciate the importance of critical thinking. I believe that analytical reasoning is a skill that formal education plays a crucial role in developing. However, school doesn't prepare us for many aspects of adulthood.

One particularly critical area is financial literacy. Many of us are thrown into managing our finances without understanding assets, liabilities, and cash flow. Despite spending 23 years in formal education, I found that I had to figure out how to manage my money and grow my wealth on my own. Dang! It wasn't easy, but with determination and persistence, I gained the knowledge and skills I needed.

When I first graduated, my priority was finding a job and starting my career. Following my path, I got a job at a tertiary hospital as a registered nurse, where I could also conduct research and publish peer-reviewed articles. Deep down, however, I knew I had to develop my investment skills and find other income sources. It would have been easy to make excuses and put these goals on hold with limited free time. But I knew I'd never achieve financial freedom if I didn't take action.

In today's world, taking charge of your money is more important than ever. There is nothing wrong with relying on a steady paycheck, but every cent counts. Even with a demanding job and a busy schedule, there are countless ways to earn additional income. The key to success is prioritising and making choices that align with your long-term goals.

Remember, the only thing standing in the way of achieving your dreams is the story you tell yourself. With diligent work, dedication, and a willingness to learn, you can achieve financial success and live the life you've always wanted. Financial planning should start when you are young rather than when you're financially ready.

> *The only thing that's keeping you from getting what you want is the story you keep telling yourself.*
> – Tony Robbins

Hold On to The Wheel

It is human nature to devote all of our energy to what you believe will produce the desired result. If you think an idea will not work out – even unconsciously – you will sabotage your potential by taking half-hearted actions. It's a direct correlation; little effort equals lousy results, which equals disheartened beliefs. It is essentially a vicious cycle in which you are trapped until you make a decision to change your mindset.

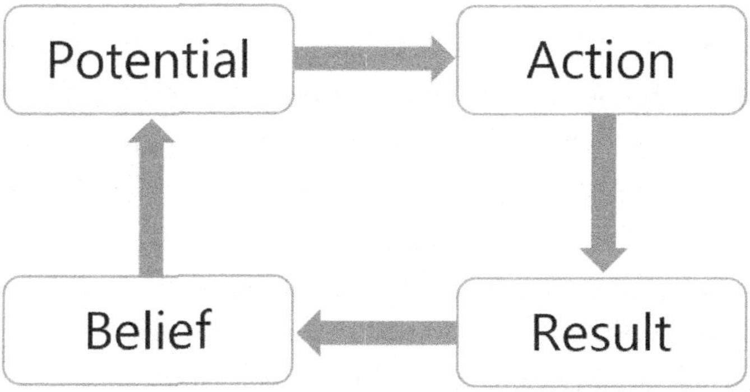

Figure 1 - Tony Robbins' Success Cycle

The Success Cycle (Figure 1) presented above illustrates Tony Robbins' key drivers of success. According to him, if a person is committed to achieving their desired outcome, they will focus and put forth more effort to accomplish it. This unleashes a person's potential and increases their confidence to take massive action. Greater actions lead to greater results.

Instead, if someone immersed themselves in negative thoughts, this could have led to a failure cycle. Beliefs can create or destroy. It tells us how much faith and confidence we should have in an idea. In most cases, our beliefs are formed unconsciously due to past pain and pleasure. Even so, the past does not determine the present – unless you hold onto it. For every belief you hold, there is an explanation. You must, however, recognise the beliefs you have created. Changing your limiting beliefs can make a huge difference!

As children in Singapore grow up, they are expected to learn two languages: English and their mother tongue. My language studies weren't great, as people who know me know. I have barely passed my English language exams since primary 3.

I have two options here. The first is to believe that I cannot do well in English and close all options that require excellent English. The other option is to remain positive and accept any opportunity to improve my English thereafter. In a nutshell, if I had drowned myself in negative thoughts of self-doubt, I would never have written this book or contributed to the medical pool of evidence-based research!

Are you willing to let your beliefs stifle your efforts toward financial independence? Are you prepared to find the ultimate opportunity to create something extraordinary – whether it is a career, personal, or family transformation?

To gain clarity, follow these four steps:

Step 1: Identify your beliefs

> Make a list of the general beliefs you feel strongly about and examine which ones are helping you grow or limiting you.

For example, if you tend to believe that you will never be successful, you need to replace that thought with an empowering one that you can be successful if you take the right actions.

Step 2: Assess your behaviour

Alternatively, you could assess your behaviour to identify why you react in a disempowering manner. That's the underlying belief in your life that limits you.

For instance, if you fear public speaking, you may believe deep down that you are not good enough to be heard and thus give up before you even try.

Step 3: Assess what you say

You may also want to consider how you speak. Have you subconsciously imposed your limiting beliefs by rejecting other people's opinions with a "but"?

For example, instead of responding to a suggestion with "That sounds like a good idea, but...", try saying "That sounds like a good idea, and...".

Step 4: Assess your challenges

Identify areas where you face constant challenges in your life. These challenges may be the by-product of limiting beliefs you have adopted as truths.

For instance, if you constantly struggle with money, it could stem from your belief that you will never be able to make enough money no matter how hard you try.

Take time to reflect on your internal dialogue to discover whether you have any negative patterns or beliefs that prevent you from achieving your goals. Once identified, you can take steps to challenge these beliefs and replace them with more empowering thoughts. In doing so, you can overcome any obstacles that are keeping you from reaching your full potential.

Key Takeaway

If you think back to your earliest childhood memories, you likely remember the times when you were fearless about trying various things. A child's curiosity can take you on a journey you never dreamed possible. However, an unending list of "social rules" piles up as we age. I once asked a friend, "What is one thing you wish you could keep if you could turn back time?"

Without hesitation, he said, "The innocence of a child's mind." The main difference between a child and an adult is that a child never limits their dreams, but an adult integrates all possible outcomes to pre-determine if their dream is realistic. That, in a way, is us creating limiting beliefs and perhaps trapping our full potential.

I want to end this chapter with a story I don't share. Even in my 30s, I still remember the day my parents argued so badly that divorce was discussed. At the time, I was only 18 years old and studying for my A levels. The process of compartmentalising my emotions, thoughts, and focus wasn't easy. I know you'll empathise with my anguish and desperation to get out and reclaim my peace if you've been through that.

In any case, my national exam score wasn't great, but I still got into the National University of Singapore. For many people, a situation like that could spell the end of their dreams. Their first step after graduation would be to find a job related to their field of study and see where life takes them.

As for me, I was determined to make my dream come true, and after years of hard work and dedication, I achieved it. Six years after holding onto my dream of being an entrepreneur, I became one.

Most people would have given up control of the wheel to be manipulated by life. But it doesn't have to be that way. Here's the key takeaway I want you to have – what you feed your mind is the prophecy of your future.

Apply this story to your life and ask yourself, are you ready to receive abundance? Are you still trapped in this downward-spiralling mindset that limits your potential? I'm not saying that your entire life is in a rut, but do you desire an outcome that you might have subconsciously sabotaged? Had you put yourself in a situation where you hoped that an external factor could have changed it?

Perhaps you are waiting for the share price to rise, your boss to appreciate your efforts, or fate to gift you the winning lottery ticket. Would you rather be the compass or the needle?

A mindset shift is unlike the resolutions we declare every New Year's Day. There's no need to start a new routine and shock the whole world; instead, try to regain control of the wheel. Make sure your wheel is straight before doing anything else.

Every successful person has a core set of habits that motivate them forward. While ordinary people think it's luck, I think it's consistency, perseverance and resilience when life repeatedly knocks you down.

CHAPTER 2

Clarity and Knowing Your Why

In most cases, it is not the outcome that matters to most people. Instead, it is the concept, idea, and vision that drives the result, which inspires, influences, and positively impacts them.

Are you truly happy with what you have achieved so far in your life? This could be in your relationships, career, finances, health or anything else. I can see many people struggling with this seemingly obvious question, and their eyes say "yes" even if they aren't.

In this chapter, I want to reassure you that there's no shame in acknowledging your vulnerability. You must embrace vulnerability as the foundation of all successful growth and achievement.

Want to see this struggle for clarity for yourself? Next time you're out for a meal, ask five random people about their life goals. In most cases, the answer will be "have more money, have a better relationship, or be in better health". Then, when you probe deeper into "Why", it's interesting to note that most people want more money because they don't want to be restricted by a lack of it. The desire for better relationships is due to the absence of disharmony at home, and the desire for better health is due to the absence of health complications.

Essentially, there are 101 things these people want to accomplish in life. The problem is, if you don't realise it yet, they usually focus on what they don't want. These people may have difficulty achieving their goals because they focus on avoiding things they don't desire. They may not be actively thinking about what they wish to accomplish, and may not be taking the necessary steps to achieve their goals.

The list of things people don't wish to achieve is as easy to regurgitate as a broken tap. It's like people are constantly thinking about and building this list. Why? Because it's true! People tend to focus more on avoiding failure than on striving for success. As a result, it is easier to come up with a list of things you don't wish to achieve than a list of things you do wish to achieve. With time, you subconsciously create a reservoir of what you don't want to accomplish to remind yourself, "Not this".

When was the last time you reminded yourself, "Yes, this is my goal in life"?

> *Your life is controlled by what you focus on.*
> – Tony Robbins

It's like when I research my next holiday trip, I must have a destination in mind. Having a destination in mind helps narrow down the research process, as it allows me to focus on the specific details relevant to that location and plan accordingly. Otherwise, I might spend a lot of time researching different locations and not making any progress. And to save myself all the hassle, I might just stay grounded in Singapore!

This concept is straightforward and applies to every aspect of our lives. Once you understand this, you'll realise how you are subconsciously jeopardising your success.

Here is another unforgiving truth about our world today: It does not matter how diligent, passionate or resilient you are. Without a clear vision of the final destination, there is no way you will ever achieve it. Period.

Gain Clarity on Your Vision

Before I ask you to take stock of your life, I need you to be honest. As mentioned, there is no shame in embracing your vulnerability. From now on, I will ask you some very challenging questions. There's no need to be politically correct or conceal your true self. Be honest with yourself if you want to keep your dreams, aspirations, and desires in sight.

Unlike my traditional Asian parents, who think mentors are just a business gimmick, I firmly believe in personal development. I have many successful mentors who I have had the opportunity to learn directly from. You may be familiar with some or all of the successful mentors I've benefited from, such as Mary Buffett, Tony Robbins, Sean Seah, and Sam Cawthorn. They all share a common characteristic – clarity of vision. It was never about how many times they failed, but the lessons learned from each failure motivated them to bounce closer towards their goals.

I know that there are many other things you could be doing besides reading this book. No matter what draws you to this book, I hope you will read it twice to soak up the essence of success. If you cannot, this chapter alone should put your life in perspective and put you above 91 percent of your peers. The same 91 percent of people who complain about life and wonder why their efforts don't translate into results.

As a professional, I hear these things too often: "I don't have enough time, Isabella, to build an alternative income source." I work at least 10 hours a day and always feel tired when I get home. While I am lucky enough to spend some time with my family over the weekends, I have a lot of competing household chores to do! Getting a side hustle is impossible for me. How can I accumulate more money so I can achieve financial freedom?"

Does that resonate with you too?

It's perfectly understandable that you think you need 36 hours of work each day to achieve a work-life balance, including creating a second income source. After all, we all want a few extra minutes each day to spend with those we care about. Nevertheless, did Elon Musk or Jeff

Bezos have more than 24 hours daily on their paths to success? It would be a blessing if this dream were true, but it's a fantasy.

Each of us shares the same 24 hours. If you think those billionaires had it easier because of luck, intelligence, and opportunity, then how about me, an ordinary girl? As a registered nurse, researcher, and investor, I worked full-time. It was certainly not easier for me than for any of you. There may have been times when I felt sorry for myself because I did not have enough time for myself. But what exactly am I trying to accomplish? What motivates me to do what I do? Have I been overworking myself just for money?

We all need some form of clarity in our lives. Clarity is like a lighthouse shining a light on a path forward, guiding us away from dangerous rocks and towards the shore. With clarity, you can better navigate the rough waters of life and find the rewards you seek. You can tell if someone is struggling with life events, having difficulty starting, or even procrastinating because they probably don't know what they are pursuing.

That's true! It is easier to waste time doing things that don't contribute to your cause when you don't know what direction you're heading in. Most clients and students tell me their goal is to accumulate more money, but money is never anyone's goal! What they're really aiming for is financial freedom and security, where money can be a tool to help them achieve it.

You have to keep an eye on the big picture regarding your finances, as this will ultimately lead to greater success and stability. After all, money is just a tool. Without a clear vision of this tool's purpose, many people earn money merely to spend it on enjoyment instead of investing it for higher returns. In my experience, this is one stark difference between extraordinary achievers and ordinary people I've met.

Roger James Hamilton, the creator of *Wealth Dynamics,* defines wealth as "Wealth isn't how much money you have. Wealth is what you're left with if you lose all your money." Without a strong wealth-generating mindset and system, all the money that flows through your hands will eventually disappear.

Have you identified what you would like to accomplish during your lifetime? When you are clear on the path you should take in life, you can spend less time on unproductive pursuits. Your dreams, goals, and aspirations become crystal clear, and a purpose drives every action you take.

Go on, write it down! Be honest with yourself – what is it that you want to achieve?

Once you have identified your goals, make sure to reinforce this image in your mind and take action to achieve them. While this book is designed to give you the knowledge and the skills to achieve your dream of being financially independent, this chapter alone will feed you the most fundamental anchor of **WHY** you do what you do. This will be the starting point for your future success.

Anchor Your WHY

The most important part of transforming your vision into reality is self-awareness. You need to understand your **WHY**.

Here are some critical WHY questions for you:

Why do you really want to rise up the ranks?

Why do you really want to take your income to the next level?

Why do you really want to start your own business?

Why do you really want to save and invest?

Did you notice how I used the words "really want"? I am sure you want to achieve many things, but at the end of the day, you must have a strong **WHY** to drive your actions. You will never give up on your dream as long as you are committed to it. By doing this, you can focus completely and stop procrastinating.

Though I consider myself a thought leader in finance, I continue to have a passion for investing, content creation, nursing, and authoring. It is almost as though I can see people's jaws dropping whenever I introduce myself. It is common for most people to struggle to find an appropriate response while trying to hide their scepticism. The typical response I receive is, "Wow, how does that work?" or "Is that even possible?"? To that, I say, "Why not?"

I'm committed to raising the status of women in finance. I believe women are equally capable, or even more capable than men in financial management. Women, too, deserve financial freedom so we can achieve whatever we dream of in life.

Let me simplify things for you. My conviction for this freedom of choice for women (why) gave me the compelling desire to raise the status of women in finance (what). The "how" came naturally as I took on every new opportunity. It is all intrinsically connected!

I know that the reasons for your **WHY** are much more profound than you think, and I will show you how to dig those out. My only request is that you prepare yourself to be unstoppable. In this process of self-actualisation, you will experience a roller coaster of emotions, and I need you to embrace this vulnerability.

You must dig deep into your heart and subconscious to discover your WHY. You shouldn't have a superficial **WHY**, such as "I want more money to achieve financial freedom". Don't forget that money is just a tool. What if you had more money? What if you've achieved financial freedom? Would this motivation be enough to keep you moving forward when life gets tough? Honestly, financial freedom doesn't address the intrinsic motivation behind why you so desperately want it.

Here's what we're finding: a deep purpose that will carry you through life's ups and downs. When life throws you a lemon, do you see a strong enough motivation to make lemonade?

I want you to ask yourself, are you driven by money or by the happiness that money brings? There is no way a tool will motivate anybody. You want the newest iPhone because of the advanced technology it provides rather than because it is just a phone for communication, right? Only when you can attach a much deeper meaning to your **WHY** will you witness miracles. Opportunities will come your way, and you will see hope. The importance of finding clarity on your path to success can't be overstated.

I first learnt about this exercise from Dean Graziosi, the author of *Millionaire Success Habits*. He called it "Seven Levels Deep", as the exercise sinks deep into your heart by asking **WHY** seven times. As Dean suggested, it's just a magical number that always works, and I second that. This exercise helped me gain absolute clarity, forming the foundation for my success today. If you need motivation to stay in check, this exercise is a great way to get you there.

The Seven Levels Deep Exercise

As an example, here is what this exercise looks like.

The purpose of my work is to raise the status of women in the male-dominated financial sector.

1st Why?

> Because females are equally capable (or even more capable) than males in financial management.

2nd Why?

> Because females are more diligent and cautious about financial planning.

3rd Why?

Because females consider every aspect of their commitments in life.

4th Why?

Because females are independent decision-makers, who should not depend on their spouses.

5th Why?

Because females should have the right to achieve their dreams and the freedom to weigh their options.

6th Why?

Arguments are inevitable in families. I can clearly remember those days when conflicts arose from differences in gender expectations. Females are traditionally expected to be homemakers and care for their families, while men work hard to make money. Unfortunately, children always get the short end of the stick.

7th why?

Even as I write this now, after so many years, this seventh "why" never fails to give me goosebumps as I get more emotionally engaged. I know for sure that I don't want to be manipulated. I am

> committed to women's empowerment in finance management because I am convinced that women should control their own lives. Women must be able to determine their fate. Whatever happens in the future, my life shouldn't be compromised, and I should be able to pursue my dreams.

When you associate a **WHY** with every decision you make, you're connecting with yourself on a deeper level to unleash your potential from within. I hope you have realised, or are starting to realise, the power of clarity in affirming your vision with a purpose-driven **WHY**.

If you have found this driving force that keeps you motivated, you are unstoppable. It is possible to shine through the gloom and flourish when others would otherwise give up. We are predestined to walk on this earth for a certain amount of time. Don't let anyone stop you from living the life you've imagined. Let no one dictate how you should live your life. Ultimately, I want you to look back in 10, 20, and 30 years and be proud of your decision today as you reaffirm yourself.

It's Your Turn Now

Throughout this chapter, I've discussed how important it is to understand your goals and motivations. Maintaining this clarity will help you stay motivated and focused as you overcome the challenges that you will inevitably encounter. We all have ups and downs after all, and life isn't supposed to be smooth sailing.

Even though you might be able to do this on your own, having a partner to hold you accountable can be extremely helpful. Having doubts and fears can keep us from moving forward as humans because our instinct is to protect ourselves. It is possible, however, to use these thoughts in a beneficial way if you use them correctly. You can make sound decisions by acknowledging these concerns and using them to inform your risk-taking decisions.

I recommend you take the time to understand your goals and motivations and then use that understanding to guide your decisions. For example, if you are considering an investment, you should weigh the potential risks associated with the investment against the potential rewards. This will enable you to make an informed decision that aligns with your goals. By doing this, you can be confident that your decisions align with your goals and values, helping you achieve your desired results.

Ultimately, success is a combination of conviction and know-how. Once you're clear on your goals and motivations, the "how" will become clearer. Embrace the things you can't control and make informed decisions about the things you can. With this approach, you'll be well on your way to achieving your goals and taking control of your life.

Of course, I understand that there's an opportunity cost in every decision we make in life. The inner devil in our heads surfaces to protect us whenever that happens. "What if I was wrong? What if I fail? What if?"

I need you to understand that this is how humans are wired; there's nothing wrong with that. You aren't crazy to have such thoughts! Again, in these moments, you should always look at your **WHY**. I want to advocate for women's empowerment in finance management because I believe women should be in control of their lives. Even though I'm not 100% successful yet, I know I'm on the right track.

What about you?

Are you ready to take absolute control of your life choices?

I've shared with you my conviction, but that's my story. It is vital that you set clear goals (what), identify your motivating factors (why) and then the "how" will flow naturally. Embrace what you cannot control and make an informed, calculated decision every time. Once you have anchored this process, you will feel powerful, as the sky is your limit.

CHAPTER 3

The Psychology of Wealth

What distinguishes the wealthy from the general public is their ability to detach emotions from mere tools. While the rich recognise money as an opportunity for the future, the general public wants to earn money for the present.

Money is just a tool. It should never be your ultimate goal in life. I have repeated this concept so many times, but it must be ingrained in your mind so that it becomes ingrained in your heart. Think about it – what is money?

The money most of us want can take two forms: a rectangular note or a round metal disc. What makes it so precious or rare? Yet, money remains valuable because people believe that it can be exchanged for goods and services.

Let's do a simple exercise. As you were walking home one day, you noticed an inconspicuous $100 bill lying somewhere on the ground. There was dirt partially covering it. Do you think it's worth picking up and keeping? You probably would! It's because you know that the value of this $100 note hasn't changed! An extra $100 could buy you a delicious dinner.

With my students, I always emphasise this one concept: "Money isn't everything, but everything needs money." Money is an essential part of our lives, and nobody can deny that. Money has the power to transform lives. And we are destined to become slaves to money from the day we are born, however.

Even Maslow's Hierarchy of Needs has its foundation in monetary transactions. Money is necessary for basic needs and medical care, as well as for more sophisticated needs such as education, entertainment, and so on. Without money, we cannot build the life we want. It is also a powerful tool that can open new doors and create opportunities that would otherwise be impossible.

Having an abundance of money can make us feel safe. This may be for this reason that some people tend to be greedier than others, as they want more than basic needs. For example, someone with a high salary might be more likely to buy luxury items like cars or expensive clothing than someone with a lower salary. Their obstinate pursuit of money traps them in the rat race, making them modern-day slaves. When it comes to money, how much is enough?

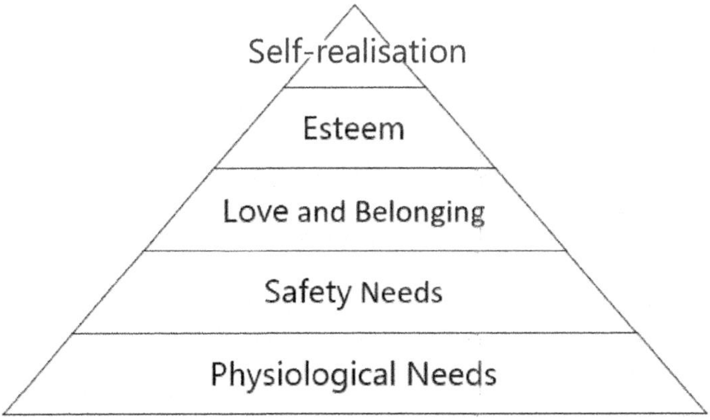

Figure 2 - Maslow's Hierarchy of Needs

In Chapter 2, I discussed how clarifying your **WHY** keeps you motivated and focused on your goal. True sense of happiness doesn't come from owning money, but rather from using it to make a difference in other people's lives. You have no idea how big the world really is. The only currency worth pursuing is humility; the only goal worth chasing is serving your **WHY**.

There may appear to be perfection in the lives of many successful and established people, drawn by fame, wealth, and relationships. As with any human being, these individuals have private pains hidden from the public eye. Do you remember the passing of Robin Williams? He was an established comedian and actor who made the world laugh, but not himself. Each story has a lesson to teach, no matter what.

Managed Well, It's A Sword; Managed Poorly, It's Just Dust

Search the internet and you'll find many successful stories of well-known individuals. Although I can use their stories to illustrate my point, the disparity in social status can make it difficult to relate to them. So here is my story.

Growing up, I was raised in a traditional Asian household where my parents believed in tough love. I can't blame them for the lack of affection, as they were raised in the aftermath of World War II. Life then wasn't easy, and they had to maximise every dollar earned for our family. Unlike how parenting is emphasised these days, my parents set boundaries in an authoritarian manner, often leaving their children to test their limits. As always, right?

Since we didn't talk about money in our family as a child, I do not recall what our family's financial situation was. To some extent, my dad has always been a man of his time – who has always made sure his family is well taken care of. In our early years, both my brother and I had a tendency to succumb to temptations. We would challenge his decisions whenever we were denied our requests. Arguments would follow, and dad would conclude by saying, "When you grow up, you'll understand". *(Honestly, I don't because I don't remember the reason for the conflict after so many years.)*

Anyway, it's just dad showing his love to us by taking care of all the problems on his own rather than making us worry. However, the lack of effective communication about money has led to multiple disagreements and conflicts within my family. As a child, I couldn't understand this.

Although it may seem hard to believe, I grew up hating money and subconsciously sabotaging myself. It was said that money is the root of all evil. It didn't make sense to me why money should be emphasised. It didn't make sense to me why all conversations revolved around money. It didn't make sense to me why these conversations couldn't be resolved amicably.

Does removing money from the equation make things better? As a young child dependent on her parents, I wasn't wealthy or rich from the start. Yet I incessantly gifted or shopped with the remainder of my allowance, allowing money to slip through my fingers carelessly. My disempowering belief system has resulted in consequences that have not served me well.

My understanding of the value of money only came when I entered nursing school. It was never about money. It's how you share your values and use this tool that's the real problem. And yet, money remains the primary way you can make a difference in your communities. *Ironic, isn't it, that nursing school taught me finance management?*

Nursing, to me, is like a lens through the silent journey of the experienced old souls who came under my care. I have witnessed the beauty, ugliness, and weakness of human beings. I can't say I've seen it all, but nursing has taught me the value of love, respect and resilience, among other things.

It is through this profession that I learned the importance of financial planning – the solution to all earthly problems. As I breathe my last breath, I want to know that I have lived a life true to myself and have positively influenced others whose paths I have crossed.

While some literature suggests nurses are desensitised to feelings, I believe the lived experiences of others deeply enlighten us. Nursing was not my chosen profession 11 years ago, but I would have chosen it all over again.

At 19, whilst still in nursing school, I started dabbling in Singapore blue-chip stocks for dividend income. Shortly after graduation, at 23, I worked on my financial safety net to ensure financial stability when my health goes south. Since then, I've invested heavily in myself to upgrade my knowledge, skills and mindset in personal finance management.

Now, at 30, I've built multiple streams of passive income through my work. I'm proud of the progress I've made in such a short period of time and I'm looking forward to further developing my passive income streams. I believe that this is the true beauty of money; it doesn't change a person, but intensifies the essence of who you truly are.

Learn To Respect Your Tool

Have you ever felt intimidated by the dramatic difference between the achievements of the wealthy and those of the average person? There's no shame in admitting that I once did! It took me a long time to feel comfortable speaking with somebody of a higher status than I was.

I mean, look at Warren Buffett, for example. In the latest news, it was reported that it cost $19 million to dine with the 91-year-old man (Alund, 2022). What! I don't think any ordinary person would have come close to having $19 million in their lifetime. This is perhaps an unrealistic, far-fetched dream.

After getting to know more influential people, I realised that we're all humans after all. We all live in the same space called Earth, breathing the same air called oxygen. How are these wealthy people different from the general public?

The difference between the wealthy and the general public can only be appreciated when you put humility above the materialistic gains of money. Humility is the first step towards greatness, where we embrace failure to learn, unlearn and relearn. Humans are born flawed, and the only constant in life is change.

In our massive and intricate world, it's always difficult to distinguish between risk and luck. Balance can only be achieved when one is able to dissociate emotions from money so that it remains an inanimate object. In this way, you can focus on what matters most to you within your sphere of influence. This is what I call the psychology of wealth.

In other words, opportunities and money abound with the right attitude and mentality. If I have learnt anything from the international bestseller, *Millionaire Next Door*, written by Thomas J. Stanley, it would be the profound respect most millionaires have for money. And I'm not talking about rocket science here. The principle of wealth is simple and foolproof, but it isn't widely practised. This is because it involves making sacrifices such as cutting back on spending and investing in assets that generate passive income. It also requires a person to be disciplined, patient and persistent in order to build a substantial amount of wealth.

> *"Money moves from those who do not manage it to those who do"*
> – Dave Ramsey

Principle #1: Don't Spend More Than You Earn

Common sense will tell you that you should never spend more than you earn.

It is likely that most millennials are unaware of the credit boom that occurred during the Great Recession. As time passes, the pain of accumulating credit debt has been effectively diluted.

In today's world, the real question is, "Who doesn't own a credit card?". The evolution of advanced payment technology is incredible; however, it can pose a more serious threat to millennials.

The "buy now, pay later" option is the newest credit gimmick that is becoming increasingly popular. In this method of payment, consumers can repay their purchases within mutually agreed upon instalment periods. It essentially generates more credit card debt if you fail to pay off this agreement. If you are not careful, the risk of default is very high, and that's where all hell breaks loose.

Make sure your money is managed in a way that helps you sleep peacefully at night. It is important not to allow yourself to fall into a spiral of debt and emotional turmoil if you ever decide to leave your job.

Principle #2: Invest in Yourself First

You will earn the greatest interest by investing in yourself.

At first glance, the term "invest" may seem intimidating to some since it typically refers to profit-driven asset classes. The reality is, we're vested in something in some way every day – just like you invested in your financial knowledge by reading this book. This concept is very simple. You are investing in your health and growth every time you watch a movie, spend time on vacation, or even practice swimming. So long as you bounce forward stronger, smarter and happier, it's an investment worth pursuing.

The good news is that unlike the mastery programs I love to attend, investing in yourself can cost you a lot or nothing at all. Whatever your level of success, it is crucial that you develop the confidence to make more significant financial commitments.

Principle #3: Embrace Calculated Risks

People who can't take risks have more to lose, don't you think?

Everything in this world comes at a price; nothing worth having comes for free. Unfortunately, not all costs come with a visible price. For greater heights, we often have to pay the price of uncertainty, doubt, fear, and regret. By defining the cost of success, we can decide if it's worth paying forward. Instead of viewing these costs as a penalty, consider them a fee rather than a cost, and you may be able to explore something completely different.

Growing Up from Zero to Hero

Let's face it, everyone wants to be successful in life. We all have our fair share of admiration for famous people and think, "How wonderful it would be if I could be like them". Our aim is to copy and model the success of millionaires, as Small Medium Companies (SMC) do with Multinational Companies (MNC). However, behind each success story is a plot that is often overlooked and underrated. Who loves to read about struggles, hardships, and sacrifices anyway? Readers always want to be inspired and encouraged, but let's be genuine here.

The path to success is often filled with many obstacles, failures, and disappointments. It is never a straight line, and it usually requires a lot of hard work, dedication, and perseverance. There can also be some difficult choices and sacrifices along the way. Being alone on this journey to success can be extremely lonely. Yes, you'll have people around you, but it'll feel different. You will have different values. You will have different goals. You will lead a different lifestyle. When you fail to keep track of what is really important, it can be difficult to carry on.

In my first contractual role as an undergraduate, my peers envied the ease of the job. The problem was that I was bored. In university, while my friends partied, I became interested in passive income. As a full-time registered nurse with a higher disposable income, I'd rather attend personal development courses than climb the nursing hierarchy. Even though my environment has changed over the years, my focus has remained the same. For this to work, you need to clearly define the game you're playing to achieve your goal and make sure your actions aren't influenced by others.

Staying committed to the fundamental principles of psychology of wealth is the only shortcut to success. It is inevitable that you will make mistakes and fail along the way. You must, however, accept the mess and embrace the obstacles. The right answer is only the one that works well for you. Take a break if you need to, then restart by learning, unlearning and relearning. Creating compounding magic over time requires that kind of endurance. Your sacrifices will eventually pay off if you persevere in this game.

The first three chapters of this book focus on the non-tangible aspects of success. Chapter 1 discusses your belief system and how you subconsciously create your reality. Chapter 2 discusses your internal fire; why you do what you do. In Chapter 3, I've discussed the psychology of wealth, humility and abundance. In order to fully utilise the strategies I will be sharing in the next chapter, it is especially important to develop the right attitude and mindset.

The time has come for you to discuss the strategies for becoming financially.

CHAPTER 4

The Success Blueprint

How we define success is different for every one of us. However, a clear definition and direction are essential to determine if we're doing things right.

Hope is not a plan, and neither is counting on the next winning lottery numbers. Up until my mid-20s, I followed this path. As I stared down the barrel of work for the next 40 years until retirement, I hoped I had invested enough to make it through retirement.

The millennial generation has a reputation for frivolous spending and is often teased for splurging on entertainment and travel. True enough, travel, electronics, and dining were my worst vices. Following graduation, I received a $3,500 starting salary, and I frequently dipped into my savings. Even after working more than 16 hours daily, there was no sign of progress in my bank account. I must say, that was quite disheartening.

Haven't you ever felt this was an unfair and judgmental comparison? The reality is that millennials are actually more financially savvy than prior generations. It is more likely that they will take risks and invest in various asset classes that can produce fast returns. For instance, millennials are more likely to invest in cryptocurrencies, which can be a more volatile asset class than stocks or bonds.

The modern world has brought millennials a lot of conveniences, but it has also presented unique challenges when it comes to money management. With easy access to credit, brokerage accounts, and other tempting investments, it can be easy to lose track of one's finances. My only wish for millennials in this modern age is for them to stay grounded in their financial planning. Budgeting, saving, and avoiding unnecessary debt are the cornerstones of any solid financial foundation.

Being financially savvy can help millennials reach their financial goals, like buying a house, starting a business, or saving for retirement. It can also save them from financial hardship in the future. While millennials have access to more information and have a greater understanding of the markets, they should make sure to do their research. They should also be sure to understand the risks associated with any investment they make. It is about diversifying risk and ensuring long-term profitability that makes up a holistic portfolio. Therefore, I urge all millennials to take charge of their financial well-being and stay grounded in their financial management.

For starters, you can use the 25x rule to estimate how much money you'll have to save to get through 30 years of retirement. This rule considers the amount you want to spend each year in retirement and multiplies it by 25. That being said, it does not account for inflation or other sources of income.

Retirement savings = Targeted annual spending x 25

As a simplified example: If you want to spend $48,000 each year upon retirement at age 65, you'll require retirement savings of $1.2 million. However, as I mentioned, this formula does not come without flaws. I highly recommend that you speak to a licensed financial consultant to assess your situation and calculate the actual retirement savings you require.

At the same time, I realised I enjoyed the freedom of being financially free, pursuing my dreams and living without regrets. There is no shame in rewarding yourself with your hard-earned money. The only question is, is your financial blueprint directing you to success or failure? How much do you understand about your financial situation?

Having a clear understanding of your financial situation gives you the ability to make smart decisions, plan for the future and understand the consequences of your spending habits. This can help you to build wealth, achieve financial freedom and ultimately, live the life you have always dreamed of.

Thomas J. Stanley, author of *The Millionaire Next Door*, suggested a simple rule of thumb to calculate our expected net worth:

$$\text{Expected net worth} = \frac{\text{Age x gross income}}{10} - \text{inheritance}$$

For example, if Annabelle, age 25, earns $60,000 per year, with an estimated return on investment of $1,000, she would multiply 25 by $61,000, then divide by 10. Her expected net worth would be $152,500. How does your net worth match up, given your age and income?

Before starting this journey, I need you to think about your financial goal and store it at the back of your mind. Focus on **WHY** you want to achieve it and **HOW** you will achieve it. Do whatever it takes!

> *It all comes down to this: If your subconscious "Financial Blueprint" is not "set" for success, nothing you learn, nothing you know, and nothing you do will make much of a difference.*
>
> – T. Harv Eker

Motion Vs. Action

Motion instead of action is often a common mistake by intelligent people – in many cases, without them ever realising it. I'm sure there are many things you want to do or want to achieve. Have you ever felt that the result of doing something was often not what you envisioned? The problem is, when you're in motion, you're constantly learning, strategising and refining. It's good that you're planning; however, this doesn't produce an actual result. Results are achieved by taking directed action.

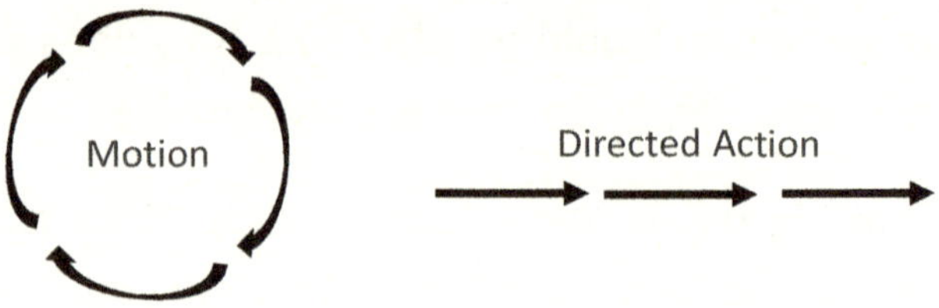

Motion instead of action is often a common mistake by intelligent people – in many cases, without them ever realising it. I'm sure there are many things you want to do or want to achieve. Have you ever felt that the result of doing something was often not what you envisioned? The problem is, when you're in motion, you're constantly learning, strategising and refining. It's admirable that you're doing something, but that doesn't generate actual results! Real results are achieved by taking directed action.

Suppose my goal is to retire comfortably by 40 years old, I should invest in business so that I can generate multiple income streams. Based on the detailed analysis I've done before, I will need to accumulate $1.7 million by the time I'm 40. Amongst other things, I'm assuming a conservative compound interest rate of 4% a year until I am 85.

Dang, this amount is unfathomable, and the fact that I have only nine years to spare isn't helping me feel any better! Luckily, I have many options to prepare for this – I can work harder, read more, attend more courses, save more, spend less, etc. The bad news is that I won't reach my goal if I stay enmeshed in my daily routine. I need to start targeting things that will generate real results – for example, spending within my budget, starting a business, diversifying my investments.

The fact that motion doesn't produce results doesn't stop us from doing it anyway. Sometimes, it helps us plan and strategise. More often than not, we do this mostly to give ourselves a false sense of security that we are accomplishing something. In this way, we can end up perpetuating ineffective strategies because we feel like we are doing something productive, despite the fact that we are actually doing nothing productive.

There's a psychological reason why people become entrenched in motion rather than engaging in directed action: they're subconsciously afraid to take risks. Many of us are experts at finding shortcuts and easy ways out. Working hard without knowing what results you will achieve is never a pleasant experience. This is like a hamster running in a wheel – it's doing a lot of work, but it's not actually getting anywhere. It's easy to become complacent and keep running the same circuits, but it takes courage and self-discipline to take the leap and try something that may lead to success, even with the risk of failure.

As you read this book, you may feel inspired and motivated. However, you will only be able to make a difference in your financial situation if you put these concepts into practice. What are you waiting for?

My One-Page Financial Blueprint

So here's my One-Page Financial Blueprint that I've developed and refined over the years. The Blueprint was inspired by Robert Kyosaki's *Cashflow Board Game*, which resembles a conglomerate financial statement. Even though some financial jargon may seem confusing at first, it's not difficult to understand. I have followed this Blueprint to manage my wealth to this day.

There are three components to my Financial Blueprint: (1) Income, (2) Balance, and (3) Cashflow. The purpose of this tool is to provide you with a broad overview of your financial health, so that you can gain insight into how you manage your finances. Whenever you're making a big financial decision, it's always a wise idea to pull out this Blueprint to see if you're overleveraging.

Profession:

Goal:

Income Statement

Income	
Description	**Cash Flow**
Expenses	
Taxes (20% per year):	
Medisave (per year)	
[Necessity] Food	
[Necessity] Transport	
[Necessity] Basic Insurance	
[Necessity] Liabilities & Bills	
Long-term saving	
Investment	
Entertainment	
Others:	

Passive Income =

(Cash flow from Dividends + Real Estate + Business)

Total Income: 0

Number of Children: 0

Per Child Expenses: N.A.

Total Expenses: $ 0.00

Monthly Cash Flow: 0

(Pay Check)

Recommendations

Description	Recommendation	Amount/mth		Actual	
Necessity	55%	0	$	0.25	
Investment	10%	0	$	0.33	
Long-term saving	10%	0	$	0.00	
Education	10%	0	$	0.25	
Entertainment	10%	0	$	0.42	
Charity	5%	0	$	45.00	

Balance Sheet

Assets				Liabilities		
CPF			**Amount**	Home Mortgage	$	0.00
Ordinary Account						
Special Account						
Medisave Account				Car Loan	$	0.00
Mutual Funds		**No. of units:**	**Cost/ unit:**			
Stocks	**Ticker**	**No. of shares:**	**Cost/ share:**			
Real Estate		**Paid-to-date**	**Value**			
Business:		**Paid-to-date**	**Value**			

Income

An income statement shows how much income an individual receives from providing goods, services, or investments. This could include wages from a job, dividends from stocks, rent payments, and any other income sources.

Balance

Balance refers to the money that is left over after all expenses are paid. This could be in the form of savings, investments, or assets. For instance, after paying for rent, groceries, utilities, and other expenses, the balance that remains in a person's bank account represents their financial stability. The number represents your net worth.

Cashflow

Cashflow is the movement of money into or out of your account that affects your liquidity. For instance, you may experience negative cashflow if you spend more than you earn.

In the next chapter, you will learn how to create your One-Page Financial Blueprint in detail. With this Success Blueprint, you can track and strategise your finances to establish strong financial health. This can be seen in the form of steady income, high investment returns, and adequate cash flow.

A Key Concept to Remember

In my experience, it is not uncommon to meet clients who often get confused between assets and liabilities, leading to considerable financial losses. To ensure that this does not happen, it is paramount to understand the differences between assets and liabilities and how they impact a person's financial stability. To simplify things, just keep in mind that **assets are what puts money in your pocket**, while **liabilities are what take it out**.

Are you aware that owning a property can be both an asset and a liability? Owning a property can be an asset, as it has the potential to generate income, such as by renting it out. However, owning a property also has associated costs, such as maintenance costs and mortgage payments, which can take money out of your pocket.

Though it is nice to be optimistic about potential future earnings, you shouldn't overleverage beyond what you can afford in the hope that it will eventually pay off. It is important to manage your finances responsibly and remain realistic about what you have to pay for. This is like a gambler going to a casino and betting more than they can afford in the hope of getting a jackpot; it is a dangerous move that can lead to serious financial difficulties. Remember, **hope is never a plan**.

Yes, I understand that financial management isn't taught in school, but you're lucky to have unlimited resources at your fingertips. As a child, I grew up around word processors, which have been replaced by giant computers that are probably displayed in museums today. Our dial-up internet connection virtually disconnected us from the rest of the world, preventing anyone from contacting us by phone. Even so, internet speeds were so slow that you would rather find another pastime instead. Growing up in the 1990s was like that.

Nevertheless, I've found my goals, motivations, and strategies through trial and error over the years. The creation of my One-Page Financial Blueprint has enabled me to gain a lot of clarity about my financial health, and I want to help you do the same. So here is my first gift to you, to help you smooth out your learning curve in holistic financial management. You can download the editable version from https://www.isabellahong.com/file-share.

This One-Page Financial Blueprint is the foundation of my wealth optimisation strategy. As Emmanuel Faber, CEO of Danone, states: "Finance without strategy is just numbers, but strategy without finance is just dreaming."

A strong financial strategy is key to achieving the goals you set for yourself – without it, you may find yourself at the mercy of your finances instead. It's like building a house without a blueprint; you may start with enthusiasm and good intentions, but without a plan in place, you'll quickly find yourself overwhelmed and off track.

Now is the time to get your own One-Page Financial Blueprint. In the next chapter, I will go over the specifics. Keep in mind that motion doesn't always translate into results. The only thing that matters is directed action!

CHAPTER 5

Creating YOUR Financial Success Blueprint

You may not have noticed it yet, but each individual holds a personalised blueprint, just waiting to be unearthed and polished for success.

In Chapter 4, I demonstrated how I manage and organise my personal finances in a systematic and simplistic manner.

In the One-Page Financial Blueprint that you should already have downloaded from (https://www.isabellahong.com/file-share), you will see three sections:

1. Income statement

In this section, we only take into account income and expenses. Make sure you enter all components to the best of your ability.

Income Statement

Income	
Description	**Cash Flow**
Expenses	
Taxes (20% per year):	
Medisave (per year)	
[Necessity] Food	
[Necessity] Transport	
[Necessity] Basic Insurance	
[Necessity] Liabilities & Bills	
Long-term saving	
Investment	
Entertainment	
Others:	

In addition, I have created an *Estimated Monthly Expenses* tab to keep track of my fixed commitments and estimate how much money I need each month. In this tab you will find information about your utility bills, insurance policies, food, and transportation expenses. Furthermore, you should categorise your insurance policies into three groups: protection, long-term savings, and investments.

+ Financial Blueprint | Estimated Monthly Expenses | Expenditure Tracking

Estimated Monthly Expenses

Categories			Remarks
▼ **Home & Utilities**	**$**	**0.00**	
▼ **Insurance Policies**	**$**	**0.00**	
▼ **Lifestyle**	**$**	**0.00**	
Total:	**$**	**0.00**	

2. *Cash Flow Statement*

This section focuses on the direction and usage of your money. Expenses for children and passive income should be entered. Other than that, everything is automated, and you don't need to do anything.

The following section of this chapter will explain how to automate these calculations.

Passive Income =

(Cash flow from Dividends + Real Estate + Business)

Total Income:		0

Number of Children:	0
Per Child Expenses:	N.A.

Total Expenses:	$	0.00

Monthly Cash Flow: *(Pay Check)*	0

3. Balance Sheet

In this section, we are only concerned with our assets and liabilities. Put them in.

Balance Sheet

Assets				Liabilities		
CPF			**Amount**	Home Mortgage	$	0.00
Ordinary Account						
Special Account						
Medisave Account				Car Loan	$	0.00
Mutual Funds		**No. of units:**	**Cost/ unit:**			
Stocks	**Ticker**	**No. of shares:**	**Cost/ share:**			
Real Estate		**Paid-to-date**	**Value**			
Business:		**Paid-to-date**	**Value**			

To keep things simple, I generally update my Financial Blueprint annually unless anything changes. However, this Financial Blueprint has served me for years without requiring any major revisions.

The only component that requires more effort will be discussed below.

Cashflow Statement

There is a new theory suggesting that forgetfulness has a functional purpose, permitting the brain to interact dynamically with the environment. Without forgetting, the brain would be too cluttered with old information to be able to process new information, making it difficult to learn new things. Though I'm not a scientist, I suppose it is a reasonable explanation for why most of us can't recall every detail of our lives.

If you ask anyone how much they spent on their meals yesterday, they probably can't give you an exact figure. And that's the problem! Unless you track your money, you will not know where it goes. Having a spending plan is therefore one of the most important lessons in finance.

Most people seeking a better understanding of their finances require a clear and visually appealing plan. Visual representations of financial information make it easier for people to identify areas in need of attention and streamline their long-term financial planning. The use of quantitative data can also help you to remain grounded since the emotional aspect of justifying your actions is taken away. Ultimately, the numbers speak for themselves!

That being said, in your personalised blueprint you should find an expense tab that you can use to track your monthly expenditures. It will automatically be input into the *Financial Blueprint* tab based on the categories you provide. If you follow those steps, you'll know if you're on the right path to financial freedom.

The Magic Formula to Remember

In terms of money, there are some things we never bargain on: food, loan repayments, and transportation. Everyday items like these are essential to our mundane lives and are functional by default. However, when it comes to spending money on ourselves, 51% of consumers reported feeling guilty (Slickdeals, 2019). In most cases, people experience guilt after realising they could have made better use of their money. Have you ever made a purchase you regretted later?

In the past, I was a student with poor financial literacy. I'd spend my allowance on comfort food or activities to feel included. Whenever I crave bubble tea, I buy it. That said, isn't it crazy that one cup of bubble tea costs S$5.30? It would be easy to get a decent meal for the same price! My spending habits back then are difficult to fathom when I look back on them.

Frugality is a virtue, but I am not suggesting you be stingy with yourself. Correct me if I'm wrong – the main objective of earning money is to spend this money with intention. For all your hard work, it's equally important to reward yourself with some money to feel good. The question then becomes how to maintain a balanced spending habit.

Emotions like greed and fear tend to influence our spending habits the most. Greed can cause people to spend beyond their means in an effort to get something they want or feel they need. Fear can cause people to spend money on things they don't necessarily need in order to feel safe or secure.

A spending plan and staying within healthy spending limits are the keys to managing our finances. You may have heard about the general 50/30/20 (50% for needs, 30% for wants and 20% for saving) rule of thumb, but I have found that most people need a less ambiguous plan. Thus, I developed a spending pot for the five main areas in which most successful people spend their money. I call it the 50/15/10/5 Rule. You can spend 50% on Essentials, 15% on Investment, 10% on Saving, 10% on Personal Development, 10% on Entertainment and 5% on Charity. This amount is calculated based on a person's monthly salary plus six months' worth of emergency funds.

*Reserve **50%** for Monthly Necessities*

In the past few years, I've taught a few friends how to manage their money and get out of debt using my strategy. Their initial responses were all condescending, "How should I manage my spending when I'm in deficit?" It's for this reason that you must prioritise your daily necessities before investing or enjoying any entertainment.

The moment you don't have enough money to cover your basic living expenses and pay off your debt, you're in trouble. I promise you, the vicious accumulation of late fees is enough to break you.

Are you aware that some credit cards charge interest at a rate of 25% per annum if you fail to pay your bill on time? For example, you have a debt of S$2,000 that you cannot repay. By paying a minimum of $50 a month on your credit card and stopping all spending, you will accrue a total credit interest of S$2,345 before it's cleared in 86.9 months. Simply put, if you own a credit card, you have to be able to pay your monthly bills. If not, don't get one!

The general rule of thumb when creating a budget is to prioritise your essential expenses first. This includes all utility bills, mortgage payments, insurance payments, and even parents' contributions.

It's adulthood now. Adulting is when you have all these bills thrown at you, and you're expected to handle them like a professional once you graduate. One way or another, I realised paying bills on time can be difficult for reasons other than money shortages. It's challenging to keep track of it all, and you may feel tempted to ignore your bills.

Arguably, the most immediate reason to pay your bills on time is to avoid late fees. It might not be clear to you now, but paying your bills on time will help you build a good credit history. This is a key factor in determining whether you will be approved for a loan. A good credit score will also mean lower interest rates and better loan terms, which can save you money in the long run.

Here, the logic is very straightforward. How would you feel about lending money to someone who is perpetually dishonest? Maybe this person is in your inner circle, and you feel obliged to help them. At the same time, you may also wish to secure some collateral to reduce your risk of non-payment. Similarly, financial companies determine their risk tolerance based on credit ratings.

You should always keep in mind that your income directly relates to your expenditures. If your income decreases, your spending habits will also need to change. Changing your financial behaviour as soon as possible will help you to emerge from your financial rut more quickly. While fast cash can be very attractive, it is never advisable to pile up credit card debt or take out new loans to meet your financial obligations. Attempt to keep your monthly necessities expenditure to 50% of your income so that you will not have to worry about a negative cash flow. Maintaining a balanced account is much easier this way.

In Chapter 6, I will discuss how to optimise your wealth through protection.

*Invest **15%** for financial growth*

The stock market has historically outperformed all other asset classes for those with an understanding of how it works. Did you know that the S&P500's average annual return over the past decade was 14.7%? This means that $10,000 invested ten years ago would be worth $39,412.52 today. Obviously, there will be winners and losers in the stock market, and nothing is guaranteed. I mean, look at Warren Buffett. As a result of the 1974 economic crisis, his net worth declined by 50%. However, look at where he is today!

Your single most powerful investment strategy as a retail investor is to increase your time horizon. The passage of time allows small things to accumulate and mistakes to fade away. Although it cannot eliminate luck and risk, it can bring people closer to their desired outcome. As an investor with 11 years of experience, I have learned that the stock market transfers wealth from the impatient to the patient.

Our goal here is to make our money work for us. All things require money, even though money isn't everything. While it is true that one of the things that cannot be purchased is time, most people are unaware that money can assist in effectively managing your time. By using money to outsource tasks that would otherwise take up a lot of your time, you can free up your time to focus on the things that matter most to you. The power and importance of financial freedom lie in the fact that slaving away for money can destroy your quality of life. Ultimately, you will want to have the option to make choices, the desire to dream, and the ability to purchase items that provide you with happiness.

There are many things that can go wrong in investing, but I assure you that it is okay to make mistakes. The stock market is an emotional chess game, and it demands a lot of emotional control to play this game well. There's one thing for sure – if you're willing to take the risk on an educated investment, the rewards far outweigh the risks. Unless you make your money work for you, inflation will lead to a decline in wealth, and it will be much harder to achieve financial freedom.

Chapter 8 will cover in detail how you can increase your wealth through investment.

*Save **10%** for long-term needs*

Have you ever felt that life sometimes strikes you hard when you are least prepared? Imagine yourself suffering from a nervous breakdown at work, and every moment spent there is excruciating. Wouldn't it be a relief to know you have the option of throwing in your resignation letter without worrying about your finances? You can also take a breather to reclaim your sanity before moving on. Saving money gives you the option of choosing from a wide range of options with peace of mind.

You do not need any particular reason to save. Just save. Life as an adult is expensive. Depending on your needs, you can save for a wedding, mortgage down payment, child or even a car. It's almost impossible to anticipate when you will need money in life because it's a continuous chain of surprises. You must understand that money doesn't magically appear when you pray for it desperately.

To be clear, I don't mean saving for an emergency fund. Your emergency fund should always have at least six months' worth of income on hand. Unless the situation is truly urgent, you should never touch your emergency fund. Aside from your emergency funds, you should save 10% of your monthly income for short-term liquidity and long-term purposes.

Our society has taught us for a long time to save. Saving is not a novel concept; however, I have seen many people having difficulties saving. In the words of Morgan Housel, author of *The Psychology of Money*, "Saving money is like the gap between your income and ego, and wealth is what you don't see." Wealth building is a strategic game plan that requires you to be faithful to your Blueprint.

In Chapter 7, I will explain how you can maximise your wealth through saving.

*Use **10%** for personal development*

You may not have noticed, but I am passionate about personal development. I felt that an aspect of personal development was lost in the shuffle that most people didn't pay enough attention to. My family and friends usually condemn me for taking personal development courses, stating, "It's too expensive". It is unfortunate that most people are more concerned about the price of a program than the benefit they will receive from it.

It's impossible to know what you don't know! Don't assume you know everything because we all have blind spots. Personal development is, therefore a process of self-awareness that enables you to better understand who you are. In this way, you can always improve by nurturing your talents and adding new skills to your arsenal, which gives you the direction and motivation to continue. A person's talent may not be evident at birth; however, it can be acquired through learning.

Investing in yourself is an investment that can pay off in the long run, as it provides you with the tools and skills necessary to excel and make a positive impression. By investing in yourself, you can unlock your potential and take control of your future. Every step forward is an opportunity to discover, explore and create something new. There's no need to wait for the Universe to turn in your favour if you proactively pitch yourself to the world. Even if you don't succeed every time, you will live a richer, more fulfilling life when you pursue your goals. As such, making the effort to invest in yourself puts you in control of your success. This puts you in control of creating the life you desire by taking the initiative to make it happen.

Personal development is the first step to achieving your full potential, and I'd allocate 10% of my monthly income to this endeavour.

*Spend **10%** on entertainment*

It is important to recognise that you, too, have needs. Even as we drudge through our mundane tasks day after day, we are still humans. If there is anything I have learned from adulthood so far, it is the importance of a first impression. Once upon a time, I thought I could dress like Steve Jobs. Nevertheless, I learned the hard way that a person's fate is determined during the first seven seconds of an encounter. Don't be afraid to spend money – buy new clothes, footwear, or even bags for yourself. For a working professional, confidence is more than innate confidence. It is also a matter of the confidence others have in you. When you carry yourself well, you will be able to boost your confidence and enhance your personality to a remarkable extent.

Happiness is your birthright. The financial demands of this life are daunting, and you have devoted countless hours to fulfilling the needs of those close to you. Spending money on people you care about can be satisfying. The majority of people, however, tend to forget about themselves. Money cannot buy happiness, yet spending money on things that give you joy in life can be extremely refreshing. This could be a fantastic book, a delicious meal, or a dream vacation. Hey, it's your life, so enjoy it! You should not be afraid to take a break from your daily routine from time to time so that you can rejuvenate and enjoy yourself.

The act of spending money can be addictive. As I have learned, it is not the act that is pleasurable but the momentary recognition and acknowledgment from the people around you that is addictive. Nursing has exposed me to numerous examples of poor financial management. In my capacity as a thought leader, I have witnessed friends and clients making poor financial decisions. Do reward yourself, but do so within the budget you have set. Whenever possible, practice delayed gratification if you do not have the budget now.

This will keep you motivated to continue with greater enthusiasm.

Spending money on yourself has many benefits. Regarding personal expenditures, I restrict my entertainment expenditures to 10% of my monthly income, but I never hesitate to spend them. Happiness will help you meet all the challenges that life throws at you. Don't be too harsh on yourself.

*Giving **5%** to charity*

Giving is an act of human connection, a manifestation of abundance. It's an act of kindness from the heart, not the brain. Several studies have found that generosity is associated with happiness, such as Park *et al.* (2017). In other words, the human brain enjoys the sense of joy more as a giver than as a recipient. Did you know that acts of charity can trigger endorphin release, resulting in a "warm glow" feeling, known as the "helper's high"?

Don't just give it; give it with sincerity. There is no feeling more authentic than when you truly believe in the cause of giving and give readily. In the Dalai Lama's view, generosity is the direct expression of our inner abundance. According to the abundance paradigm, there is enough for everyone; the key is to cooperate with the Universe to help and share with others. There will eventually come a time in your life when the Law of Attraction will bless your life in unexpected ways.

There is true manifestation in the Universe; whatever comes around goes around. The method of giving does not matter; you can give your time, effort, or money, whatever suits you best. A thoughtful gift can have a greater impact than a gift for the sake of giving. While I have food on my plate, water in my cup, and shelter over my head today, many others do not. If I can contribute 5% of my monthly income, why not?

The best advice I can give you is to detach yourself from your emotional attachment to money. As I have stated numerous times, money is merely a tool. Take advantage of this tool in order to enhance the happiness of others so their happiness will be reflected in yours in a positive feedback loop. While you may not receive the love presented by the Universe immediately, you will receive it sooner or later. In life, everything you do has a cause and an effect. The manifestation of abundance might surprise you one day when you least expected it.

Simplify And Automate

If you find it difficult to stick to a spending plan, you aren't alone. In reality, there are several different budgeting strategies, but the 50/30/20 rule is probably the most common. I developed the 50/15/10/5 rule because it aligns reasonably well with my core values. This way, I have the motivation to stay committed to my plan.

This is intended to be your personalised Financial Blueprint. Be sure to align your spending plan with your values. I place great importance on the five expenditure categories in my spending plan, and I intend to fulfil them. It does not, however, imply that I will spend every penny as planned. After paying my monthly bills, it certainly doesn't hurt to save up or invest any excess funds I may have. Choose what is best for you! Keep your spending within your budget at all times.

The most important thing is to avoid reinventing the wheel and complicating things. The simpler the process, the more likely you are to follow through. In fact, you might find it helpful to think of each pot as a regular bill to be paid. To make this work, you would need to open four additional bank accounts and set up automated transfers between these accounts on payday. You should only withdraw funds from your respective accounts to pay your bills. While it may seem old-fashioned, keeping track manually every month gives me a sense of accountability; it allows me to reflect on what I can eliminate or reduce. Despite this, you should not spend more than one hour per month on this process.

I hope you have been able to follow through with your Financial Success Blueprint. The Financial Success Blueprint has provided me with a great deal of financial stability, and I hope it will do the same for you. By doing so, you can gain a better understanding of how much you earn, what you own, what you owe, how far you are from your goals, and where your money is located.

Conquer this gateway to financial freedom, and you'll breeze through the rest. To be honest, the path to financial freedom is straightforward, but believing and maintaining a consistent approach will require conscious effort.

CHAPTER 6

Protect What's Yours

In sports, there is a famous gameplay strategy that states, "The best defence is always a good offence". How true is this in the field of finance?

The task of juggling your financial obligations may require you to cultivate a zen-like calm – *namaste*. You may have student loans to pay, a mortgage, a car loan, parents to support, and a newborn to care for. As a result of so many ongoing commitments, you may find yourself spread too thin financially. In fact, my experience has brought me to the realisation that wealth protection is often not given the priority it deserves when people are barely surviving. Many individuals view wealth protection as an indulgence that they will do when they have more money at their disposal.

On the other hand, it's always interesting to hear the same group of people talk about things like wealth accumulation and wealth creation. We all want more money, right? As a huge fan of these topics, I could literally talk about them all day – so stay tuned for the next few chapters! But first, let's talk about wealth protection now. Wealth protection is essential, no matter what your circumstances are, and I would be remiss if I underplayed its significance.

A successful financial future depends on the protection of your wealth. Simply put, if you want to achieve financial independence one day, you've got to protect your wealth. I'm pretty sure nobody is ready to lose all their wealth and start over. Certainly not the rich, and never average people like us. As small as our sacrifices are now, we can't afford to face adversity like a severe illness or enforced retirement that could wipe out our savings. Leaving your wealth unprotected could cost you money that you'll regret for the rest of your life.

The etymology of "wealth" comes from the older English word "wel", which means happiness, prosperity, and well-being. Throughout history, it has morphed into modern-day riches and prosperity. With that in mind, it's time to reclaim the true meaning of "wealth protection"! It's not just about protecting our own money, but at the same time we'll also protect the happiness and welfare of those we love.

Wealth protection includes many personal finance strategies such as insurance, asset preservation and tax reduction. It sounds simple, but you must consider the opportunity costs of each strategy to ensure that you do not spend more than you can afford. Living in deficit with an empty bank account will put you a few steps further away from financial freedom. In other words, you need to take charge of your wealth!

Insurance

At some point in our lives, we all want to achieve financial freedom. In order to keep ourselves financially stable, many of us believe that saving and investing are sufficient methods. The policies purchased for the purposes of protection, saving, and investing are not interchangeable and should never be mixed. Years ago, I thought my whole life policy could double as a savings plan. I now realise I'd be foolish to surrender my insurance policies for quick cash. It makes no sense to double up on insurance as a saving plan when there are plenty of better-paying options available!

Insurance is a powerful tool used to protect yourself financially in the event of an unexpected loss. It provides a financial safety net in case of an accident, illness, or other unexpected event that could result in a significant financial burden. The concept of health and medical insurance encompasses four aspects (see diagram below). These are non-overlapping coverages that provide coverage for four different scenarios: diagnosis of critical illness, income replacement, accident coverage, and hospitalisation coverage. I will leave the specifics to your financial advisors since this is not meant to be financial advice. Understanding the different types of insurance is important so you can pick what suits you best.

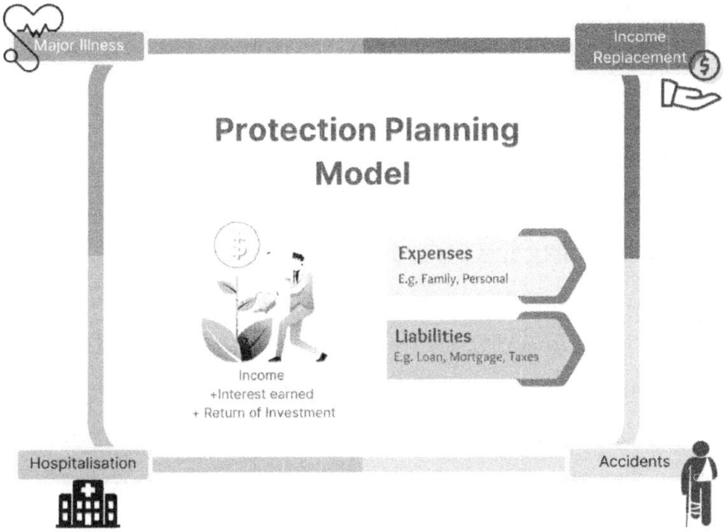

Financial planning is incomplete without the purchase of insurance, as it provides financial security in the event of any crisis in life. Each policy is meant to achieve a specific goal or purpose. Millennials have been quoted as saying, "Buy term, invest the rest". Have you ever wondered whether that is truly the best option for you? Sure, term insurance is cheaper, and the excess can be reinvested. As an ardent investor myself, I thought I would be in favour of this strategy. However, I'm not convinced by this statement.

First of all, let's be clear about why you're buying this policy. Insurance is supposed to protect you, so don't try to make money out of it. Secondly, ask yourself whether this coverage is meant to be a long-term or short-term solution. Lastly, do you have a cash flow problem that might stop you from paying your premiums? This clarity in itself will guide you to the answer you need.

As an example, suppose you wish to protect your family from inheriting your outstanding mortgage debt – you'll purchase mortgage insurance. A term plan should do the trick since Singapore's maximum loan tenure is 65 years of age. On the contrary, if you're looking to protect your life – you'll purchase whole life insurance. Since you can't predict when things will happen, you can't prepare for them. The idea is to make a conscious decision to transfer the financial risk away from you so that those you care about will be secure no matter what happens.

A common mistake is to assume that you have the luxury of time and youth on your side. No matter where you are in life, you will need insurance coverage at some point. However, the younger generations do not seem too enthusiastic about discussing insurance coverage. These are years of premium commitment, but we don't know when we'll "enjoy" these benefits. But what if we don't? While most peer-reviewed medical journals suggest that major illnesses are more likely to occur as we age, aren't we able to wait to purchase insurance later in life?

Although insurance is not something many people want to think about, we should ask whether we also have the blessing of lady luck? A growing number of studies have revealed that severe illnesses are becoming more common among younger people. The choice is clear: should you gamble on being insured with a lower premium and peace of mind, or should you risk being uninsured with a substantial financial burden and a higher premium? In this regard, it is similar to the idea behind the purchase of lottery tickets – hope. The state of our health cannot be predicted, but we need assurance that our well-being is well taken care of.

There will never be an end to the commitments you have. As ironic as it may seem, the more financially strapped you are, the greater the need for insurance. However, when you look at life from a practical perspective, you'd probably realise that the only certainty is illness and death. Day-to-day life involves risk; we can choke while eating, slip while walking, or even contract COVID-19 while socialising. Insurance is a must unless you intend to save specifically for unforeseeable medical expenses.

A commitment is made with every insurance policy purchased. This means that you shouldn't give up on your policies for any reason. Always make sure your insurance policy is within your budget before you commit. Whenever cash flow is a concern, prioritise the problems to be resolved first and speak with your financial advisor periodically. As a general rule, you shouldn't spend more than 15% of your salary on insurance premiums. This fund should come from your necessity fund, of course.

Asset Preservation

Asset preservation is an essential financial planning strategy that is mostly known by wealthy individuals. As the name implies, asset preservation is a strategy that protects one's wealth from creditors' claims. When debtors have few assets, the traditional approach may be more advantageous than initiating proactive asset preservation measures. This makes sense because the cost of preserving assets may outweigh the potential benefits in such cases. Whenever you talk about asset preservation, the spotlight is always on the rich and famous. Haven't you heard about the infamous celebrity prenuptial agreements between Brad Pitt and Angelina Jolie or Kim Kardashian and Kanye West that surprised the world?

As far as I know, asset preservation isn't just for the rich and famous. The truth is that everyone possesses assets that they wish to preserve as much as possible. There are a lot of things that can add risk to your life, like business risks, family issues, and taxes. Even though what we have to preserve may not be worth billions today, it is equally important to accumulate and grow for a financially secure future. Determining whether a proactive asset preservation approach is appropriate depends on the value of your assets and your willingness to take risks. You can benefit from the help of an asset preservation attorney or a specialised financial consultant in this regard. Make sure you don't spend more than you can afford.

Here you're creating an asset preservation strategy so you can protect your assets without engaging in illegal concealment or fraud practices. A successful asset preservation plan starts with an assessment of your assets and their risk factors. For instance, if you have real estate that is increasing in value, you may want to consider transferring it to a trust or other entity to protect it from creditors or lawsuits.

The same can be said for your profession. Your profession can also impact the level of risk you are exposed to and the type and method of asset preservation strategies that you should employ. For instance, a doctor may be exposed to malpractice suits, while a lawyer may face professional negligence claims, and a consultant may face breach of contract claims. Therefore, it is important for you to understand the risks associated with your particular profession and implement the necessary asset preservation strategies to protect yourself and your business.

If you have been procrastinating about asset preservation, now is the time to seriously consider your options. You could end up in a sticky situation that you could have avoided due to your procrastination. It is okay to take your time to contemplate during times of crisis. You must, however, determine your next course of action. Keeping your assets secure is not only important for short-term defence, but also for long-term security.

Tax Reduction

Do you know that January is one of my favourite months while April is one of my least favourite? At the start of the New Year, I consider January a crucial month for setting my pace and setting goals for the rest of the year. Plus, it's my birthday month! Jokes aside – April is my least favourite month since it is the time when I have to file my taxes and contribute to the CPF (Central Provision Fund). Could you imagine how ironic it is thinking I should be thankful for high income taxes since they mean "I've performed well"?

Income tax is one of the most popular forms of taxation and is an important component of a country's revenue generation. For Singapore to be known as the Green City, who do you believe funded all the roadwork and greenery that exists today? Once again, adulthood has imposed a set of responsibilities on us that we cannot ignore. The only times I wish I was born in a country with no income tax are during times such as these.

As obligatory taxpayers, it is our responsibility to make sure that we do not overpay or underpay. Singapore's individual income tax rates follow a progressive system. This means that the tax rate is calculated according to your income as long as you earn at least SG$30,000 per year. To add to that, with a higher income, you are expected to pay a higher tax rate. Welcome to financial responsibility!

Robert Kiyosaki, the author of *Rich Dad, Poor Dad*, once suggested that he doesn't pay taxes. The wealthy don't either. Here's the million-dollar question – **HOW**? That's the biggest question. Even though there are a lot of reports about the rich evading taxes, I don't endorse it. Remember that tax evasion is a criminal offence. Can you even avoid paying taxes? The quick answer is yes – if you understand how money can be used intelligently.

In the broader context, we could dig deep to examine employee and business owners' characteristics. As a nurse, I was paid a fixed monthly salary in return for my time and effort. I was subject to income tax on the monthly salary that I received. As a business owner today, my income is distributed between two funds:

Business and Personal. Taxes will only be charged on the balance after business expenses.

COMPARISON

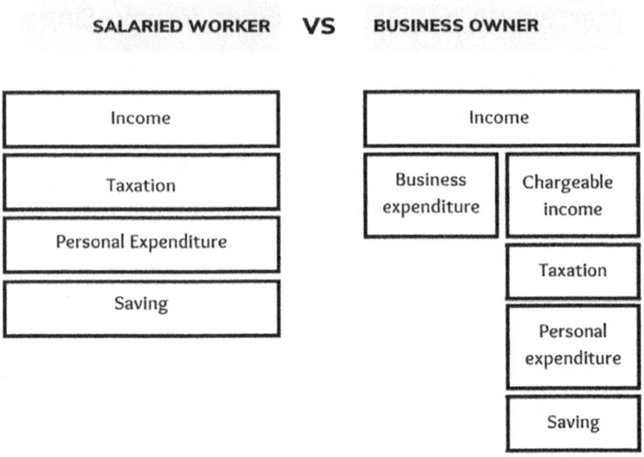

For instance, I can deduct my business expenses, such as marketing costs and utilities, from my gross income before I pay income tax on the remainder. This concept is similar to Robert Kiyosaki's *Cashflow Quadrant,* which explains how the rich get richer. Likewise, he believes wealth transfers from those who trade their youth for money (left) to those who leverage a proven system (right). I like that Singapore doesn't tax capital gains from investments, unlike many other countries. Yay!

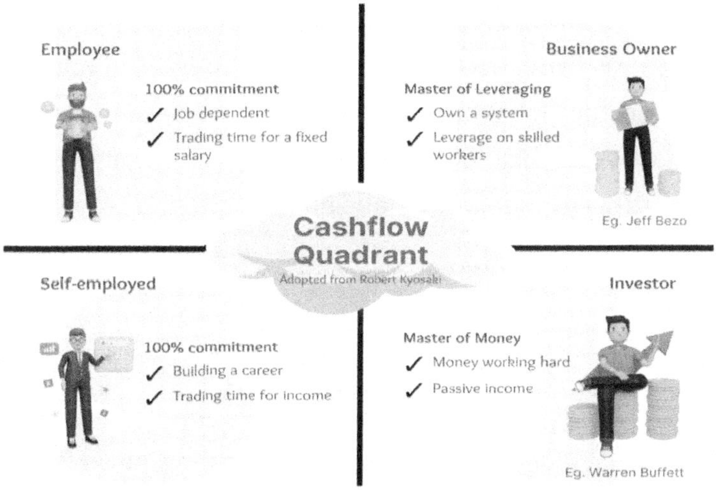

Besides, you should research what tax relief, rebates, and deductions you can take advantage of in your own country. One of the biggest mistakes I made as an employee was thinking e-filing was automatic and I didn't need to get involved. It wasn't until I was forced to file my income tax that I realised how much I had been overpaying. For your reference, the Inland Revenue Authority of Singapore (IRAS) has a transparent structure. Singaporeans can learn more about tax reliefs, rebates, and deductions by visiting IRAS's website.

A one-size-fits-all approach to finance does not exist, and tax savings will vary based on the circumstances of each taxpayer. Taxpayers should take into consideration their financial goals and risk tolerance. They may want to consider other options, such as investing in specific types of tax-advantaged accounts, that could potentially offer greater returns than just tax savings alone. Ultimately, it is important to weigh the pros and cons of each strategy and decide which one is best for you personally. To that end, always seek a financial consultant's advice for clarity.

The Honest Truth

It may have become clear to you from reading so far that financial planning can be approached very systematically. The process shouldn't be too complicated after all. A sound financial plan can be created by anyone with the right knowledge to reach their goals and secure their financial future. The process does not take much time and effort. It just takes a bit of dedication and patience.

Today, financial planning has been made more accessible so that everyone has an equal chance of becoming financially independent. You can learn the basics of financial planning by reading books, taking online courses, or even listening to podcasts. By doing so, everyone can achieve their financial goals and secure a brighter future. With so much information readily available online, finding answers is not difficult. Having said that, how competent are you at managing your money?

Taking control of your financial future with an accountability buddy is something I've always admired. We all have egos, which make it difficult for us to appear weak and vulnerable to others. And people tend to be reserved about finances because it is a sensitive and sacred aspect of their lives. Accepting an accountability buddy shows that you are willing to open up, listen, and take charge of your finances.

Accountability buddies can be anyone, but they must be someone whose knowledge you can trust. I love working with my financial consultant. Yes, I also have a financial consultant! Emotions are innate to humans, and you can't get rid of them no matter how hard you try. There are times when you know what is right in theory, but you cannot help but be swayed by your own emotions. Thus, having an accountability buddy can help keep you on track and focused on what is most appropriate for your current situation.

In most cases, the greatest obstacle to achieving a breakthrough is the execution of the plan. Having said that, execution entails opportunity cost, "loss of money," and commitment. These are generally the things that most people are afraid of and most concerned about. *“Could I get a better deal somewhere else? Are you going to charge me again? How long until I can stop paying?"* Don't you ever think that before making a big decision? Truthfully, I believe taking a leap of faith takes a great deal of courage.

If we genuinely care for the people we care about, keeping our wealth protected is not an option but a necessity. It is important, however, to recognise that every commitment entails a certain degree of responsibility. Before making any decision, it is imperative that you thoroughly evaluate the financial and personal circumstances of your life to ensure that they are purposeful and based on your best interests. In finance, you don't want to attack without a solid foundation that can crumble.

Congratulations on mastering the first stage of personal wealth management. The next chapter will reveal my secret to infinite savings.

CHAPTER 7

The Secret of an Infinite Savings Loop

Financial literacy is a skill. A person who understands the value of money will then be able to master the science and art behind the game of money.

My best gift to my 21-year-old self was to embrace the comfort of stepping out of my comfort zone. That year, I lived with my cousin in Australia for two months during my mid-year break. I was so grateful that she accommodated my visit while she was studying and working part-time. While she was busy, there were pockets of time to fill, and I had to be self-reliant.

It's still fresh in my mind how anxious I felt when I walked down the slope behind her hostel to grab a Subway sandwich by myself for the first time. It was a mixture of exhilaration and fear of being alone for the FIRST TIME in my life.

What happens if I get lost? Will people judge me for eating alone?

My mind was filled with many negative thoughts, but the moment I stepped outside, these thoughts dissipated in the cool evening breeze. That's when I fell in love with being alone – reflective, yet not lonely.

The experiences I have had while travelling solo have been among the most memorable of my life. Solo travel for me relates more to the sense of accomplishment and personal fulfilment than to the destination. Maybe only those who embrace their vulnerabilities and love themselves first can understand this. Like an addict, I'm addicted to this feeling of accomplishment. I used to travel every quarter when I was an undergraduate, and now I do it every other month.

My love of travelling has evoked two reactions: envy and concern. My friends envy my ability to travel while they're stuck in Singapore with debts and responsibilities. My more mature friends, however, worry about my safety as a solo female traveller and doubt my financial management skills. I could tell from their questions, like "How are you going to afford such an expensive lifestyle?" My parents also advised me to save money.

There's No Straight Road to Success

It is a surefire way to invite trouble if you delay saving until later in life. Delaying saving can have a compounding effect on your financial future. The earlier you start saving, the more time you get to save because you are earning more and hopefully have fewer financial obligations. With age, you may lose your ability to earn more money and have more conflicting financial priorities, making it harder to save and plan for retirement.

Money is not going to appear out of nowhere when you need it most. Believe me – it won't! The practice of diligently saving requires a long-term commitment and consistent effort. You can start an infinite savings loop no matter where you are in life, but it will take some sacrifices. I speak from experience when I say that the result is worth it. The earlier you start, the more time you'll have to save, invest, and grow your money. You don't want to wait until it's too late!

Humility and a growth mindset are essential for mastery in any field, so don't fall into the trap of thinking you know everything. Sweetness is only discovered when bitterness is tasted. There would be no colour without black and white. Knowledge is a powerful force, but it is often crushed by these three words – "I know that". And here's the problem: you cannot know what you do not know! Although saving is a simple concept, it should be approached deliberately. Simply stashing money away without a plan will not assure your financial security in the future.

The traditional method of saving money in a bank account is no longer ideal, as annual inflation can erode the value of your savings over time. With annual inflation of 2.5 – 3% on average, your savings accounts and fixed deposits will never be able to recuperate their losses. If you're not happy about saving $100,000 for 20 years only to withdraw $54,000 afterwards, please listen to what I have to say.

My goal in writing this book is to broaden your understanding of finance and personal wealth optimisation. I want to see you succeed! Living a financially independent life doesn't mean giving up what you love. It means being able to pursue your passions and spend time with the people who matter most to you. By implementing a deliberate strategy and consistently working hard, you can achieve financial independence and enjoy the things that are truly important to you.

The New Wave of Saving

The *Cambridge Dictionary* explains saving as "to keep something, especially money, for use in the future". In a financial sense, it simply refers to income not spent and kept safe. As mentioned in Chapter 4, you should set aside at least six months' worth of emergency funds and consistently save 10% of your monthly income. Certainly, there is no more enticing temptation than instant gratification, with dreams of quick cash and high profits. However, let's be realistic. Savings shouldn't be subjected to any significant risks since they will be the only sources of funds available during a recession. Now, the question is, what can you do to maximise your savings to avoid inflation's horrors?

Let me introduce you to a new concept of saving: saving by generating income. You may be wondering what I am talking about. What are some of the ways in which we can generate additional income from our savings, other than investing it? The performance of investment vehicles is volatile, unpredictable, and unreliable. We cannot be sure that our savings will be spared during bear markets, so how safe is it to put them in any investment vehicle? What if the market collapses when I am most in need of funds? Are you out of your mind to suggest this?

Oh, phew. It's a relief to know you're actively thinking about what I'm about to say instead of just believing everything I say. Would you like to know what every successful individual has in common? It is their independent ability to analyse, evaluate, and implement a proven strategy based on logical reasoning and a great deal of effort. Be proud of the fact that you are on the right path to success!

Think of dressing well as an investment in your first impression, eating well as an investment in your health, and continuing education as an investment in your knowledge. It is the same concept. The efficient use of savings could have also been regarded as an investment. In essence, you wish to save intelligently so that your savings can outpace inflation or, at the very least, be on par with inflation while exposing yourself to minimal risk. As a player in the financial world, you must recognise when it is appropriate to take risks and when it is not.

Are you aware that there are many asset classes in which you can invest with minimal risks? Take a moment to consider this. As Singaporeans, we are fortunate to have the Central Provision Fund (CPF), which provides interest rates of between 2.5% and 4% annually. From a **SAVINGS** perspective, this fund isn't too bad.

In addition, Singapore Saving Bonds (SSB), Treasury Bonds (T-Bills) and Singapore Government Securities (SGS) are fully backed by the government with a AAA rating. In other words, you are almost certain not to lose your investment unless the Singapore government fails.

Other options, such as fixed deposits, endowments and gold, are perhaps not as safe as those described above, but they carry lower risks. The Singapore Blue Chips may also provide you with a dividend income if you prefer a higher level of risk. Unlike many other countries, dividends are not taxable in Singapore! You may also consider investing in rental property as another means of creating an Infinite Savings Loop.

Remember, you should ensure that your emergency funds are easily accessible. You should also strive to maximise your savings so you can achieve an Infinite Savings Loop.

When you are ready, here is how I established mine.

My Secrets Revealed

As a 19-year-old undergraduate student, I realised that I would have to plan if I ever wanted to live comfortably in retirement. The world will not wait for you to make your mark. Inflation is not an unfamiliar phenomenon; Singapore's inflation typically runs between 2-3% per year, but it hit 22.4% during the 1970s economic depression. As most of us have not experienced a real economic crisis, 2022 may be the beginning of the next major recession if it is not handled properly.

Now, how many of us have sufficient savings to withstand a major recession? Or perhaps we could ask how many of us have salaries that increase proportionately to the rising cost of living.

In the midst of a world full of temptations, it is humanly impossible to be free from all earthly passions and desires. What fun is it to drown yourself in work just to make a living? How does it feel to be unable to do what you love and need only to save money?

My goal here is to empower you to live a fulfilling life. I have a long shopping list, but before I pull out my credit card to make a purchase, I always ask myself three questions:

1. Do I really need this now?
2. Can this wait?
3. Can I gain any value from this?

Imagine you have been eyeing a classic black top for quite some time, and it is now 30% off in the Black Friday sales! Most people would recognise that the price is lower than usual, making it a great purchase! There is no better time to own this timeless piece! That is how marketing can capitalise on the weakness of human emotions. Unless you have a solid strategy for managing your funds, you will fall victim to your emotions. Let's face it, what matters is not the price of the top but how much emotional control you have.

My wealth mindset would, however, inform me that I would still have to pay 70% for the timeless piece. Certainly, it is cheaper than before, and I have been eyeing it for a considerable time. However, is it truly necessary for me to purchase this piece now? Has my spending been within my budget? If I were to purchase this, how would it add value to my life? *Keep in mind that your non-essential expenditures should not exceed 10% of your monthly salary (see Chapter 4).* This method is effective! Many times, I skip the deals after much deliberation. Having 70% of the cost at my disposal does not make me miserable, but rather happier!

Friends may not always agree with you, and it is not your responsibility to please them. I used to have friends teasing me about my frugality, but guess what – I DON'T CARE one bit! Stick with your Blueprint for Wealth and enjoy the results. Rather than living paycheck to paycheck, I am confident that you will be much happier creating your own Infinite Savings Loop.

This is probably the most exciting part. What's the best way to close this Loop of Infinite Savings? There's nothing exciting about saving the traditional way. Growing up, my mom always deposited my Ang Pows (red packets) blessed on my birthday and Chinese New Year in my bank account. The interest I earned was probably less than 1%, but I was too immature to figure out what it meant. But, it feels great to have the cash when I started taking control of my finances at 19.

A decision I made when I was 19 and living on campus changed the course of my financial future. Instead of engaging in the typical college social scene, I committed my time and resources to learning about finance and investing. With no background in finance, I set up a regular savings plan to invest in Singapore ETFs (Exchange Traded Funds) and stocks. Even though I knew that investing involved some risk, I was willing to take a calculated risk in order to achieve higher returns.

As a young, frugal person looking back, I realise this was one of my most courageous decisions. My Infinite Savings Loop was created through reinvesting dividends and generating passive income to ensure my financial stability. Whenever you are unsure about taking a risk, just remember that sometimes the most courageous decisions lead to the best outcomes.

The only regret I have now is not starting my endowment policy earlier. I was first introduced to endowment policies during my university years. As I recall, I was sceptical about endowments at that time. Why would I lock up my money for a significant period of time only to earn a meagre 4% a year? My argument was that I could easily get more than 10% per year on my investment through the stock market! It took me 11 years to appreciate the value of an endowment. As much as we desire growth, we must also ensure that there is an adequate financial safety net. Endowments are a great way to ensure financial security as it not only provides steady returns but also protect your original investment.

Working in the financial industry has made me aware of the importance of segregating my money deliberately. As a rule, our savings portfolio should be kept safe as opposed to being a gamble on the outlook of the economy. My naiveté and youth at the time led me to be confused between the two strategies. Even at 30 years old, investing a portion of your income in a long-term savings plan is better than none. Ultimately, your goal is to ensure you have access to adequate financial resources regardless of economic conditions. What a turn of events for me!

Myths Debunked

This new wave of saving offers many more possibilities than traditional methods if you give it a chance. My father told me one of his friends is terminally ill and is concerned about the financial well-being of his family. Upon his death, he could potentially receive a CPF payout of SG$300,000. This amount, however, is insufficient to feed a young family of three. Before I continue, I would like you to identify where the problem lies. Could this be a current issue – insufficient resources to meet the family's day-to-day needs? Or is this a future problem – for how long can the family survive on this SG$300,000? Surely the answer is obvious.

So, here it is: when the primary breadwinner passes away, the family will receive a lump sum of SG$300,000. For a short period of time, the family would no longer have to worry about their daily necessities. There is, however, no way to predict how long this amount will last. It is, therefore, important for everyone to have a financial plan in order to live comfortably.

In response, my father questioned whether it was feasible for them to invest this money in order to solve the family's long-term needs when they were barely able to make ends meet. His question was, "*How comfortable do you think the widow would be with parting with the money she received for her family that is barely sufficient?*"

Now, the onus is not on others but on the widow herself – if she can detach herself from the emotional attachment she may have to money. Here's one possible solution to consider. Having no debt, the family may not require so much liquidity at any given time. The widow could save a portion of the fund she received in order to create an Infinite Savings Loop for her family's future. It is imperative that she maintains her foresight and carefully considers which asset classes are appropriate for her circumstances.

In this regard, I would like to emphasise that you do not need as much liquidity as you think you do. By implementing an appropriate Wealth Blueprint, you are in effect living within your means. The savings you consciously set aside for long-term planning are a valuable asset. It's unlikely you'll run into any cash flow problems if carefully strategised.

In finance, success is not determined by right or wrong strategies but by learning from mistakes. A wealthy individual's mind is forward-looking, while a poor individual's mind is stuck in the present. By understanding the underlying mechanics of the game of finance and learning from their mistakes, you can increase your chances of success. Having a few setbacks on the way to regaining your motivation is normal at this point; most people experience some setbacks before getting back on track. Don't give up, and keep pushing forward.

You have successfully completed the second stage of mastering personal wealth management. Stay tuned for the next chapter, where I will reveal my secret to investing safely.

CHAPTER 8

Keep Investing Simple

People give up on investing for two reasons: they lose money, or they lose patience. In reality, they are missing out on an opportunity to achieve financial independence.

Although I committed to financial freedom in 2011, it feels like yesterday. Before then, I was that typical entitled millennial who didn't care about anything. Yet, the global financial crisis that shocked the world in 2008 touched a nerve in me. At the time, I was just 16 years old and was not vested in the stock market. My heart sank when I saw the economic foundation shaken as adults around me whispered, "This time is different". People who were vested in the stock market were trapped. Can you imagine CITI Bank's stock price dipping 98% to its lowest point in history? I told myself that I would never touch the stock market.

Yet, in my naiveté, I didn't realise I'd begin investing three years later at 19. What were you doing when you were 19? I was just an ordinary nursing student at the National University of Singapore. Although I was happy to have money in my bank account, I couldn't help but wonder how I could nurture it. As a matter of fact, even if I did nothing with this nest egg, inflation would still rise between 2 and 3% a year! To ensure that my money kept up with inflation, I began to research investing and financial planning. Little did I know that this decision would set me on the path to financial freedom.

You can't achieve *Financial Freedom and Retire Early* by doing nothing. Nursing has exposed me to the pretty, the ugly, the rich, and the poor. My patients have shared many stories with me, revealing differences in their attitudes towards money management when they were younger. As a result, their lifestyles are drastically different between the wealthy and the underprivileged. And I decided – I wanted to live with dignity, not charity. That is what motivated me to invest in my future at a young age, taking control of my financial future.

The concept of investing has existed for millennia, and there have undoubtedly been many critics throughout history. Many successful investors have been made famous through their investment attempts, such as Warren Buffett and Charlie Munger. However, bankruptcy and family disruption have also been reported due to investing. It may be luck, but I believe that 90% of success is attributed to knowledge and discipline.

Before I continue, let me address the three most common criticisms of investing:

1. Investing is risky; you can make significant gains and big losses.
2. Investing is non-guaranteed; you might not get your capital back at the end of the day.

3. Investing is too difficult and too complicated.

Investing poses real concerns, and I never intended to demoralise you by exposing them. Let's be honest about this. Your goal is to earn money, and mine is to assist you in achieving financial independence. Investments involve inherent risks, and no one should be under the illusion that they will get quick cash from investing. I will address your biggest concerns in the following chapters.

I do not know what you have learned about investing or what you believe you know about investing. I encourage you to set aside your preconceived notions about investing and keep an open mind as you read what I have to share. Learn, unlearn, and relearn – let's start over from scratch. By investing, I seek to create an alternative source of income through passive income and long-term growth. You'll need to think like a business owner and pay attention to just three elements: Risk, Reward and Time horizon.

Start With an Intention In Mind

When I turned 21, I decided to take charge of my finances and invest more actively. Having no background in finance, I am not sure how to start and where to start. Whenever my dad took me to investing seminars, I was so bored because I couldn't understand a word. It is as if they are speaking a different language. Starting with the basics, the first book I read was *3 Dimensions of Successful Investing* by the Securities Investors Association Singapore in collaboration with Singapore Management University. The book gave me a basic understanding of the foundations of the various asset classes.

Investments can be made in a wide range of financial asset classes. Depending on your preferences and goals, investments can be made in stocks, bonds, mutual funds, exchange-traded funds, commodities, real estate, and other specialised asset classes. Each has its own advantages and disadvantages and should be considered alongside your risk tolerance and financial objectives.

Over time, I developed my own investing framework, which I call E.P.S.I. (**E**arn, **P**rotect, **S**ave, **I**nvest). Investing is a long-term endeavour, and it should be kept as straightforward and simple as possible. To date, I have used this framework to generate two outcomes: (1) passive income, and (2) long-term growth.

To make money work hard for you, you must first have money. The first step is to study hard, find a decent job, and accumulate money. With your salary, take 15% of your earnings to invest in your protection (Chapter 6), save 10% for your infinity savings loop (Chapter 7), and invest 15% to accumulate wealth over the long term (Chapter 9).

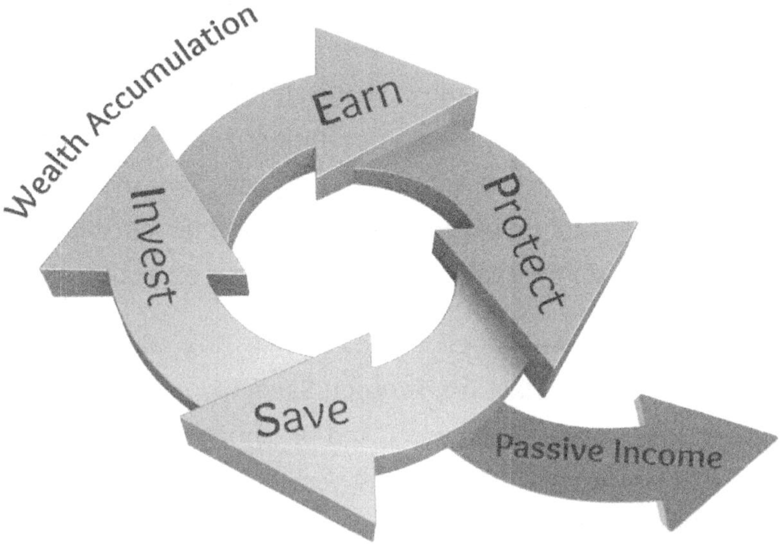

I invest primarily in U.S. stocks as it is the most efficient means of achieving long-term financial success. The U.S. stock market has historically outperformed other forms of investment, such as bonds and real estate. It does not require a large amount of capital to begin investing, and it offers a greater degree of flexibility in relation to inflation protection.

Have you ever been unsure whether it makes sense to invest in mutual funds? After all, these funds were meticulously designed by professional fund managers to beat the market but rarely succeed in doing so. What is even more annoying is that investors must pay for the services of professionals regardless of whether they perform as promised. In his book, *Unshakeable*, Tony Robbins suggests that overpaying for mutual funds is one of the most costly mistakes in investing. He advocates investing in index funds instead.

Contrary to this, I prefer to mitigate my risk by investing in a mutual fund as a means of diversification. With mutual funds, you can spread your investment risks across a variety of investment classes and geographic regions. Even though index funds have the advantage of a low-cost investment, mutual funds allow you to benefit from different economic conditions while still maintaining a balanced portfolio. Additionally, mutual funds can provide a steady income stream through dividends.

Discovering Your Personality: Investing Vs Trading

In Chapter 7, I discussed my foray into the Singapore equity market at 19 years of age as a higher-risk saving method. People who are familiar with the Singapore stock market scene might notice that the local exchange exhibits lower volatility and capital appreciation than the U.S. exchange. It was so boring to see very little progress in my portfolio! The only thing I liked about Singapore is that dividends are not taxable.

After graduating with higher spending power, I decided to improve my investment skills by investing in myself. I began with value investing and then ventured into technical trading on the U.S. market to maximise my profits. I had no patience in the stock market, and all I can think about is quick money. My trading journey was full of excitement and a heck of a ride – I kid you not.

I was a nurse by day, and I spent my nights hawking the U.S. stock market. As the saying goes, "sleep is for the weak." I slept an average of four hours a night. Let's use simple moving averages, MACD, RSI etc. Could there be a continuation of bullish momentum or perhaps a reversal in the trend? There were so many ways to interpret a simple white chart filled with green and red candlesticks. It did not matter which direction the market was trending; my emotions were high. In my own words, I call this the Deception of Trading Psychology.

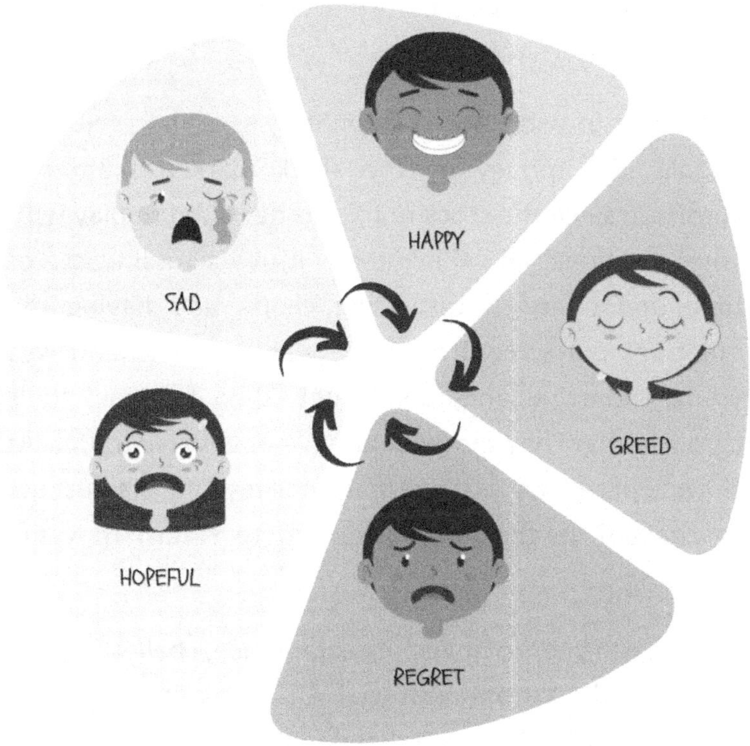

When you become entangled in the Deception of Trading Psychology, you lose control of your emotions. You'll feel good when the market's on your side. And there is this inner voice (greed) that whispers, "Wait a bit longer before selling". Now, the price briefly retraces within a split second after gaining momentum. You instantly regret it – why didn't you sell earlier? You pray that the stock price will rise, but it is too late! The market has turned its back on you. What would you do? Most people would cut their losses before it drops further. And the cycle repeats.

According to widespread estimates, as many as 90% of people lose money on the stock market. I am not surprised since the stock market is designed to play with your emotions. As I think about it, it's a total waste of time and energy interpreting charts and having my emotions out of control. There was a time when I was young and naive, and I don't think I'll do it again. I don't care whether I had more favourable or adverse trades. At the end of the day, is it worth leaving my financial success to chance? In the end, I decided to return to value investing.

After seven years of investing experience, I believed I had mastered the art of investing. I was on a mission to look for fundamentally sound companies to buy below their intrinsic value. A single problem remained: it is extremely difficult to find a value stock during a period of a bull market. Only after meeting seasoned investors like Mary Buffett and Sean Seah in 2018 did I realise there was more to learn. Their investing philosophy, along with their guidance, has kept me on a grounded path ever since.

A key investing concept you need to understand is that investors do not pick stocks. Investors pick businesses. In every good business, you will find that solving people's problems is at the heart of their mission, guided by a strong leadership team. According to the latest data from the US Bureau of Labour Statistics, only 35.5% of businesses succeed after ten years. In light of this, how can we determine whether a business will remain successful during a period of economic crisis?

Before you throw in your hard-earned money, you must analyse if it fulfils the criteria below:

- Solid business model
- Honest management leadership
- Equitable valuation

As an investor, like any business owner, you cannot expect it to grow by itself. You should review the fundamentals of the company periodically unless you are invested in an index fund. You should also invest with a systematic framework to reinforce your conviction and confidence in investing.

Go to www.isabellahong.com/services to learn more about this framework.

Investing Game Plan

In my professional career, optimising my clients' wealth has always been one of my key interests and strengths. I guess it's not surprising since *Analytical* and *Futuristic* were listed as my top five strengths in Gallup's CliftonStrengths Assessment. As I see it, you should have a clear understanding of your investment objective and strategy – why are you investing? How are you investing?

The first step to creating your investing game plan is understanding your wealth psychology, your limiting beliefs, **WHYs** and your relationship with money (Chapters 1-3). The second step is to create a spending plan for money allocation (Chapters 4 and 5). Earlier, I introduced the E.P.S.I. framework as a guide for guiding investment strategies, which you can check out in Chapters 6-9. Last but not least, Chapter 10 discusses the management of your investment portfolio.

Your ultimate goal is to create passive income and accumulate long-term wealth. To do this, you'll want to diversify your portfolio to include a mix of low-risk and high-return investments. While every asset class comes with different risks, you need to know what each has to offer before investing. You'll also want to consider how much risk you're comfortable taking and how long you're willing to wait for your investments to mature. Investing in stocks is inherently risky, therefore, avoid leverage to avoid being trapped in a margin call during a market downturn. Last but not least, you will need a plan for reinvesting your profits in order to grow your portfolio over time.

Embrace Mistakes and Learn From Them

Hey! Whether you are a new or experienced investor, I want you to know that mistakes are normal. Allow yourself to make mistakes now, while you are still young and energetic, rather than later in life when you cannot afford them. However, if anyone tells you that the investing industry is rosy and that it is guaranteed to be profitable, run away from them! Take flight! There have been various instances of investing scams, and I do not want you to be their next victim. Even Warren Buffett, the Oracle of Omaha, cannot guarantee that any investment will be profitable, and he, too, has made mistakes along the way!

Over the course of my 11 years of investing experience, I have made my fair share of mistakes. There have been times when I have lost foresight in my analysis and made a loss in my investment. Mistakes are nothing more than lessons to be learned. My mentor, Sean Seah, has made mistakes during his investment career. The same can be said for his mentor, Mary Buffett. In the end, it is your ability to bounce back from mistakes that is most important.

In my effort to impact as many lives as possible by providing them with the knowledge to manage their finances and maximise their wealth, I have noticed that there are a few common themes that are prevalent among my mentees. Here, I will be completely transparent and brutally honest about my experience because I sincerely want you to achieve financial freedom. I apologise if you feel hurt, but I look forward to receiving your appreciation once you reach your first million.

Don't Chase Money. Attract It.

I always enjoy beginning my investing bootcamp by gaining an understanding of my mentee's wealth mindset. In most cases, I ask, "What are your goals for attending this three-day bootcamp?" The intent here is not to understand their expectations from the course but what success means to them. They usually respond the same way every time: *FINANCIAL FREEDOM, RETIRE EARLY*!

This is the problem: many people falsely believe that investing is the key to financial freedom and early retirement. I would like to clarify that this is not exactly true. Investing can help you achieve financial independence through passive income, but you will need to keep investing to increase your wealth in retirement. The growth of your investment portfolio requires you to maintain an active income. "Retire early" is an idyllic dream that people idolise. But let's be realistic.

People in this group are also often attracted to fast profits. However, investing is about building wealth through investment in good businesses and the compounding effect of time. In order to achieve success in trading, you must be disciplined and undaunted by emotions. The best advice I can give you after experiencing a great deal of emotional turmoil is to ground yourself. In the long run, your mental health should not be compromised by instant gratification.

The key to financial freedom and retiring early is to live a fulfilling and purposeful life. Do your best and believe that money will come to you if you work hard. In Chapter 3, I repeatedly stressed that money is only a tool that can be used to help you achieve your dreams. The pursuit of money is not a dream in and of itself. I believe this concept applies to all aspects of life. Consider the scenario in which you are chasing after your crush. There is a delicate balance to be struck here – if you are too aggressive, they will be scared off.

With money, we can pursue our dreams and passions, but without purpose, it can cause stress and frustration. By having a clear sense of purpose, we can focus and motivate ourselves to save for retirement, make smart financial decisions, and, ultimately, achieve financial independence. Doing what you love and helping as many people as possible is a truly rewarding experience. Although money is necessary, it cannot be compared with the youthful energy and health you currently enjoy.

This Time Is Different; No, It's Not.

I believe that the stock market is primarily logical, contrary to popular belief. Companies that are publicly listed are subject to rigorous audits and are required to disclose their financial information on a regular basis. As investors, it is our responsibility to perform due diligence and analyse these numbers. A stock market can, however, also be manipulated by powerful individuals for their own advantage, often by playing on our emotional responses.

Despite strong underlying data and financials, a single tweet or news article may trigger a dramatic shift in market sentiment, making it difficult to predict market movements. This is why it is crucial to remain informed and not allow our emotions to cloud our judgement when investing. You can avoid falling victim to undue market volatility by taking a measured approach and analysing both the fundamentals as well as the broader market trends.

In the world of investing, the four most dangerous words are "this time is different". Apart from the literal changes in time, what makes it so different now from what it used to be? Each financial crisis has the same characteristics – employee reductions, decreased corporate profits, and gloomy economic prospects.

There are some good businesses that can attest to time, while there are others that cannot. The thing is, if you invest in fundamentally sound companies, you don't even have to worry about their longevity. Truth is, nothing's changed except our emotions.

A couple of years ago, I decided to try my luck in Las Vegas. As soon as I won a couple of hands, I thought I had lady luck on my side. The tables changed suddenly, and there was a whisper in my heart that said, "This time will be different. Let's try again." Needless to say, I lost entirely because of my recklessness.

In essence, if you enter the market blindly without first understanding the concept of investing, you are gambling. Donating to charity can be done in a number of ways, and the stock market is certainly not one of them. Having no idea what you are doing is a gamble that can leave you vulnerable and helpless in an emergency.

> *You never know who is swimming naked*
> *until the tide goes out.*
> *– Warren Buffett*

The bull market makes everyone look like a genius, but only the bear market reveals the truth. One more relevant example is the transient economic crash caused by the closure of global borders due to COVID-19 in 2020.

In the words of Warren Buffett, "Buy when people are fearful, sell when people are greedy". While the market was bottoming out, I noticed a flurry of investing "experts" appearing on my social media accounts. As a matter of fact, the stock market never moves in a straight line, so what goes down will often come back up. Indeed, the bull run that followed the global reopening was a delight. I saw an increase of at least threefold in my portfolio. However, all these "experts' disappeared when the tables turned in 2021.

There will be no difference between this economic crash and any other. If only you could step away from your vested interests to see the truth. As the earth rotates, the sun rises from the east to the west. The business world continues to operate, and transactions continue to take place.

There is only one difference between the two: your state of mind. It may be that you are unfamiliar with the concept of investing, or you have failed to do proper portfolio sizing, which has resulted in emotional distress. Keep in mind that if you do not know what you are doing, you will never be at peace.

You Can Invest Alone, But You'll Do Better In A Community.

As a beginner investor, I spent the first five years of my investment journey trying to figure out the whole concept on my own. At that age, I could not understand the language my dad and brother used, and none of my friends were investors.This meant that I had to rely on traditional and digital resources to learn on my own. Over time, I was able to gain a better understanding of the investment process and develop my own strategy.

When the market was on my side, I felt confident and comfortable. When the market was against me, however, it never showed mercy to me. Self-doubt arose from time to time – could I have been the problem? *What have I done wrong? Am I not suited for investing?* It was a lonely journey without anyone with whom I could share, support, and celebrate.

Investing in myself gave me the opportunity to meet more like-minded individuals who are as passionate about investing as I am. As the "odd-one-out" for a long time, it was a relief to know I was no longer alone. By surrounding myself with a vibrant community, I have been challenged to improve my investing skills. It was like Charlie Munger to Warren Buffett.

There is much in common between my story and yours, isn't there? Although the concept of investing has existed for millennia, people continue to repeat the same mistakes. Even today, I make mistakes. I would have made more mistakes if it had not been for my fellow investors, who held me accountable. I recommend you join a tight-knit community in which you can discuss and analyse companies and give each other support.

CHAPTER 9

My Investing Strategy Revealed

The whole essence of investing is to buy shares in a fundamentally sound company at a reasonable price at the right time to make money.

I have always believed that it is important to invest in oneself first. Since I graduated from the National University of Singapore and started my first job in 2015, I have sought out investing classes to improve my knowledge of the field. For my knowledge of the stock market, I have taken courses on value investing, options investing, technical analysis, and arbitrage trading. The amount I have spent learning about stock investing alone could be estimated at SG$19,000 over a period of seven years. This does not include all of the personal development and property investment courses I have attended, which could easily add another SG$50,000 to this figure.

What's on your mind right now? Like most of my friends, I know you're thinking, "Oh, hell no, girl!" How can you be so generous with your finances? Where does it come from? ” Like all of you, I maintain a full-time career and lead an honest life. I worked hard, created a spending plan, and stuck to it.

As you may recall, in Chapter 3 of my Wealth Blueprint, I recommended that you allocate 10% of your monthly income to self-education. Specifically, I am referring to courses in personal development. However, in my professional capacity, I have observed that the majority of people have little interest in personal development. It saddens me to hear this as personal development has had a significant impact on my life. While formal education emphasises knowledge and critical thinking skills, personal development emphasises skills and knowledge necessary to succeed in the real world. We all desire financial independence in life, do we not?

In addition, time does not wait for anyone. The most appropriate time to learn or improve a skill does not exist. There's no excuse not to do anything; *I'm too old, I'm too young, I'm too...* Snap out of it! Your only excuse is what you have permitted yourself to believe. Although I sometimes stood out as the youngest student in the personal development classes I attended, I never let my young age hinder my ambition to succeed. That is how much I am committed to achieving success. How about you?

You're Who You Think You Are

For too long, I allowed myself to believe that I was not born to run. Everyone knows that running is my greatest weakness, and I am not afraid to admit it. Back in school, I competed in 100- and 200-metre sprints for my house, and I usually placed within the top three. However, I have always dreaded taking the National Physical Fitness Award (NPFA) exam. When it came to the NPFA test, I consistently performed at the bottom of those who found it difficult to pass.

The only way I was going to pass the test was by training. I have trained in parks and attempted to hit the treadmill countless times, but it rarely lasted more than ten minutes. During the experience, I felt my heart pumping outside of my body, my muscles tense, and my lungs gasping for breath. And that was pretty much the end of my training session. The more I trained, the more my subconscious convinced me I was just challenging the impossible. It was a challenging endeavour.

In six years of primary school, I struggled through my 1.6 km run.

In the four years of secondary school, I took shortcuts to complete my 2.4 km run.

Things were more stringent in the two years of junior college, and there wasn't an easy way out. I had to attempt the 2.4km test several times before finally passing. I went through hell.

Who would have thought I would be training for a half marathon today?

Have you ever felt trapped, unable to move beyond your current circumstances? Perhaps you have been striving hard to climb the corporate ladder, but promotion doesn't come your way. Despite your best efforts, you have not been able to achieve a breakthrough with your investments.

If this is how you are feeling, I must tell you that your subconscious mind is sabotaging your efforts to achieve financial freedom. The same was true for me – I believed that I wasn't born to run. I allowed myself to be trapped by a self-limiting belief that I had constructed to justify my failure.

You will be more successful if you find a role model who inspires you. How do they think, behave, and act? My turning point came in 2022 when I participated in the Standard Chartered Marathon Run for the first time in my life. While my training was brief, what changed was not my goal to compete in 10 km but a conscious change of mindset. The role model I looked up to was a friend who broke through with her slender frame to become a triathlete. I felt more motivated to match her success than trying to meet some specific checkpoint that had no meaning to me.

In the same way, Warren Buffett is my role model when it comes to investing. The investment strategy that he follows is very straightforward and straightforward - he invests in fundamentally sound businesses that are run by honest and capable individuals at a reasonable price. The volatility of the market day-to-day does not bother him since he aims to be a long-term collector of good businesses.

You should not expect the journey to be smooth and easy. The beginning is always tough, and it's where most people start being creative. My success in achieving financial freedom was not achieved by seeking fast profits. Instead, I focused on "becoming" Warren Buffett to mimic his thought processes and attract passive income along the way. Whenever I entered a position, I pondered what Warren Buffett would do and asked myself whether my thesis was substantiated.

Who is the role model who really inspires you?

The M.N.T. Strategy Revealed

I am a minimalist who prefers to keep things simple. Even after 11 years of experience, I still prefer Warren Buffett's investing style to all other strategies I have learned. His strategy focuses on three things: (1) the business model, (2) the management leadership, and (3) the valuation.

These data are mostly objective and straightforward, and they do not require any imaginative interpretation. I did not need to monitor the market movements, and I enjoyed a healthier lifestyle as a result.

In the event that the stock market was to go on hiatus for ten years, I would not be concerned about my portfolio.

Additionally, Warren Buffett typically invests in well-established and highly profitable companies. His investment strategy is limited to companies within his circle of competency, which he can analyse and evaluate from a business owner's perspective.

In other words, he doesn't usually invest in fancy growth companies that rely on transformation and development due to the unknowns. Rather than speculating on the future of a business, he has always objectively analysed and calculated its growth potential. It's my belief that this gave him the confidence and conviction to invest billions of dollars.

Fortunately or unfortunately, technology has become an integral part of our lives during this time of rapid transformation and growth. Technology advancement is a hot topic among young people, and I understand why. Anyone would be tempted by a golden landmine hidden by the underdog, right?

The problem is that many of these companies have yet to demonstrate their financial stability through a proven track record. Furthermore, the recent bull market has resulted in an overvaluation of most technological companies. A financial crisis could cause many of these companies to collapse if it is not carefully managed.

If you are so confident and convinced about your thesis that you are willing to take calculated risks, what should you do? With stable companies, it is easy to become bored. Growth companies, however, present a much greater risk. In the same way that all investors desire growth, all business owners desire profit. This is when I began to think, why do fundamental and technical analysis have to operate separately? Why can't I take Buffettology a notch higher by investing in fundamentally strong companies at the right time? Hence, my M.N.T. strategy was born.

The M.N.T. strategy aims to invest in fundamentally strong companies alongside bullish market momentum. What goes higher in a bullish momentum will go higher. What goes lower in a bearish momentum will go lower. It does not, however, imply that the market cannot move in the opposite direction. In this case, your objective is to catch the reversal in trend and enter or exit a fundamentally strong company at the appropriate time. Using fundamental and technical analysis in conjunction has systematically assisted me in determining when to enter a trade by averaging costs and when to take profits.

Macroeconomy

Is there ever a time when you feel as though the market works against you when you place a position? As soon as you invest in a promising company, the market turns against you, resulting in significant losses. It is actually quite frustrating, I know. It is important to understand, however, that macroeconomic conditions can be unpredictable and can often work against your best interests.

Several years ago, I met someone who said the market will rebound after every significant intra-day drop. Occasionally, this is true, but not always. The probability of this statement being true is 50-50. So, I thought, how can I make investing more objective and systematic so that retail investors can make their own decisions?

In order to address this issue, it is important to understand the rationale behind market volatility. There are times when market swings are simply knee-jerk reactions by manipulators, and other times when they represent a fundamental shift in the market. When market fundamentals have been shaken, it may not be the best time to fight against the trend and force an entry into the market. There is always the possibility of dropping even lower!

An understanding of macroeconomics is essential to making informed investment decisions. You should monitor the market and be aware of any potential changes that may affect your position. If the market fundamentals have shifted, it's best to wait until the dust has settled before entering. A good strategy is to remain patient and wait for the right opportunity.

Here are a few examples that I will be actively looking for as a starting point:

- Geographical politics
- Affairs of state
- Supply and demand
- Interest rates and inflation

Net Worth

My investment philosophy is based on Buffett's value investing philosophy of identifying companies that are fundamentally sound. This was briefly described in Chapter 8, where you were asked first to analyse if the company satisfies the following criteria:

- Solid business model
- Honest management and leadership

- Equitable valuation.

Here, let me provide you with a more detailed explanation.

Our goal in evaluating a business model is to determine how a company generates profits. Investors are ultimately owners of a business as shareholders. As any business owner would, you will want to see your business profitable. I look out for the following components:

- Operational structure
- Sustainable comparative advantage
- Business risk.

When evaluating management leadership, I aim to determine how well the management is leading the organisation. The importance of trust and rules cannot be overstated in any organisation. We all make mistakes from time to time; while mistakes in business are inevitable, personal misconduct is not tolerated. In my evaluation, I consider the following factors:

- Governance structure
- Management goals and strategies
- Financial performance
- Red flags.

When evaluating a company's valuation, our objective is to determine its value. I look for indicators that indicate an overvaluation or undervaluation of the company. There are many models of analysis available, including discounted cash flows or intrinsic calculators. For myself, I simplified the process by comparing the price-to-book ratio and price-to-earnings ratio over the past ten years to determine if it's discounted.

By understanding these factors, you can make more confident and informed investment decisions. A thorough analysis of a company's fundamentals can help you identify promising investments and minimise your risks, resulting in long-term success in your investing endeavours.

Timing

Technical analysis can help you identify trends and changes in momentum in the market. These trends and changes can help you decide when to buy and when to sell. By combining value investing and market analysis, you can maximise your returns from the stock market. Nevertheless, it is imperative to keep in mind that predicting the market accurately is nearly impossible due to emotional factors and manipulation.

The key is to understand and appreciate the market's volatility and to develop a strategy that works well for you. The retail investor may find it more advantageous to wait for an upward trend before entering a position. The reason for this is that dollar-cost averaging during market dips can quickly deplete a company's available capital.

Investors must remember that investing is both a science of strategy and an art of emotion. There is no one-size-fits-all strategy that will work for everybody. Take the time to test it out, and develop your own investment style that suits your risk tolerance. Additionally, do your due diligence, take calculated risks, and never go against the trend since you cannot beat the market. The key to long-term success lies in understanding and investing with patience and discipline.

The bottom line is that I used the M.N.T. strategy to guide my investing approach. As a first step, I will always study the macroeconomic outlook in order to understand the risks associated with investing in the market. Secondly, I adhere to Buffett's value investing philosophy, which identifies companies that possess sound fundamentals. As a final step, I also analyse the momentum of the market to identify opportunities for entry and exit.

CHAPTER 10

An Abundance of Golden Goose Eggs

Wealth optimisation is a process of continuous refinement to build a fundamentally strong portfolio that profits regardless of market volatility. The goal is to use our finite resources to build a fortified infinite income stream that withstands all economic conditions.

Almost eleven years ago, when I started investing, the stock market was viewed with fear and trepidation. The stock market offers no guarantees, and everyone has the potential to either win big or lose everything. I remember – whenever I initiated a conversation about investing, my peers condescendingly responded with, "Hey, you're 19! What do you know?" Little did I expect that even the most conservative group of friends would be investing in the stock market today! In my curiosity, I often ask them what has changed; and the most common response has been, "Just trying it out ".

Ironically, the same group of friends became more defensive when presented with the idea of developing a well-balanced portfolio. There are 101 things that they may be concerned about, such as the lock-in period, break-even point, capital guarantee, capital appreciation, charges, etc. I find it interesting, however, that they are willing to take a chance on the stock market but not with a balanced portfolio. As everyone knows, it is more dangerous to invest in the stock market if you do not understand what you are doing. Investing in the stock market may give you the impression that you are in control, but retail investors have no control over the market's direction.

The investing world is experiencing a great deal of hype these days, and I understand why. The seeds that our parents sowed have produced a generation of millennials enjoying higher education and comfort in their lives. Particularly with the advent of cryptocurrencies and web 3.0, investing has become increasingly popular among millennials. Also, technological advances have made investing much more convenient and accessible to consumers today.

Unfortunately, this hype can be misleading. It is important to remember that investing in the stock market is still a risky endeavour. It is important to do your research and understand the risks associated with investing before diving in.

To illustrate, I have a love-hate relationship with the aggressive marketing tactics used by brokerage firms to attract clients. In an effort to attract clients, I have observed brokerage companies offering free shares or a "zero-commission" policy. I mean, is there anyone who does not find promotional offers appealing? Any promotional offer should, however, be read carefully. It is probably common knowledge that anything that appears too good to be true most likely is. You should make sure you understand what you are signing up for.

Investing is a strategy game, a test of character, and a long-term commitment. The only way to become financially independent is to play this financial game with a proven plan. In the words of Warren Buffett, "Be greedy when the market is fearful, and fearful when it is greedy." This must be understood within the proper context. His confidence arises from investing in fundamentally sound businesses managed by honest leaders at a decent valuation. Because of ignorance, I have witnessed many friends losing money on the stock market. Therefore, please do not invest out of fear of missing out.

The key to achieving financial freedom as an ordinary young woman is to diversify my portfolio and manage it effectively. It is absurdly possible for a millionaire to invest a lump sum and receive a passive income of $3,000 per month. But what are the chances of an average income earner replicating this strategy? How can you ensure that adversity does not adversely affect your wealth plan and your dreams? The purpose of this chapter is to show you how to profit effectively regardless of the volatility of the market.

Diversifying Your Portfolio

In my professional capacity, I strive for (1) long-term growth and (2) income generation in all portfolios I design. Among the biggest misconceptions I've noticed is that many people believe the US stock market is the easiest way to achieve financial freedom. Well, I'm not surprised since this is how most marketing strategies market investing. In fact, I was once blinded by the greed for capital appreciation because I didn't fully understand what financial freedom is.

As we all know, the average annualised return of the Standard & Poor's 500 Index (S&P 500) from 1957-2021 is 11.88%. By the effect of compounding interest, we would have accumulated slightly less than $1.5 million if we had invested $1,000 from the get-go. Isn't that great? Nevertheless, if we had withdrawn $100 per annum for income, this amount would have been reduced by 84% to slightly over $200,000. Ultimately, to achieve financial independence, you need a portfolio that generates both income and long-term growth.

For too long, it has been assumed that young people are more likely to tolerate higher risks because they have a longer timeframe to deal with volatility. Though logical, this statement ignores the emotional fluctuation that occurs during difficult times. Theoretically, we all know what to do, but in practice, we are all a little confused. It is not pleasant to see a deficit in one's portfolio, is it? You have to find out how to unleash the full potential of all kinds of financial assets.

Whatever your level of risk appetite, a balance must be achieved somewhere. A person with a high-risk appetite may concentrate on the stock market and balance it with mutual funds. Conversely, those with a lower risk appetite may focus on mutual funds and balance them with bonds. *Have you heard the saying that you shouldn't put all your eggs in one basket?* With this strategy, you can benefit from both capital appreciation and dividend growth at an acceptable risk level.

Here is a case study I presented with Mary Buffett, the ex-daughter-in-law of Warren Buffett.

Look at Microsoft Corporation (MSFT) from 2011-2022:

- An average of 2% p.a. dividend yield,
- Capital appreciation of 797% over the past 12 years.

For an investment of US$10,000 made in 2011, you could expect capital appreciation of US$79,700 and interest of US$8,000 by the end of 2022. In any case, I wouldn't be too bothered by the dividends received as dividends paid by U.S. companies are highly taxed at 10 – 37%. It is no wonder that Mary Buffett suggested that the Buffett family doesn't pay taxes on their portfolio as they would choose to reinvest all dividends received.

In my evolving understanding of the financial markets, my general rule of thumb is to always strive for long-term growth and income generation. In terms of long-term growth, I consider the U.S. equity market to be my first choice. In order to generate income, I will turn to mutual funds. Choosing mutual funds to balance my portfolio risk is due to the dedicated risk management offered by professional fund managers. Even though the fees are slightly higher, they compensate for the risks I am about to take. The world does not offer free lunches, as we all know.

Concentrating Your Vested Interest

Millennials today live much easier lives than their forefathers did. How many of you have been through a major setback before? As an example, here is a case study. How would you feel if you had grown your portfolio from US$5000 to US$34,000,000 over 29 years, only to have your net worth decrease by 50% at the age of 44? As it turns out, Warren Buffett did! The Oracle of Omaha is known for his tenacity in bouncing back after setbacks.

As a matter of fact, every financial crisis is followed by worldwide reports of panic. For example, after the 2008 financial crisis, many people had to liquidate their portfolios, and many experienced severe depression as a result. Similarly, some investors took advantage of the 2008 financial crisis to purchase high-quality stocks at low prices, leading to large returns later. Self-made millionaires are also known to be born during financial crises.

The stock market has historically provided the highest return on investment of any asset class. I have heard a variety of perspectives during the course of my 11-year investment journey. There are those who believe that diversification dilutes a portfolio, while there are others who believe that concentration is the key to massive wealth growth. Warren Buffett once said that *"diversification preserves wealth; concentration builds it".*

The field of finance does not have a right or wrong strategy. Instead, it has a strategy that is suitable for you, and that has the potential to generate consistent profits over the long term. If you stop to think about it, has any sector of the stock market been untouched by the financial crisis? The majority of you are probably too young to have experienced any major global financial crisis. You may, however, recall the most recent transient COVID-19 crash.

While some sectors performed better than others, no sector was spared. Does diversifying within the stock market make any difference here? Nope! Owning multiple stocks on an exchange does not necessarily imply a well-diversified portfolio but one that is chaotic. Unless you're a full-time investor, there's no way you can keep track of every corporation's activities and reports. Instead, your investment strategy should remain focused and only invest in companies within the scope of your expertise.

Consider diversifying your stock portfolio in the S&P 500 index if you plan to own multiple stocks. The S&P 500 index consists of 500 leading public companies based on their market capitalisation. Research is not required, and monitoring is easier. With a longer time horizon, you would be better off using index funds to ride out the volatility of the stock market.

My strategy in portfolio management has always been to diversify my money into multiple asset classes so that I can capitalise on the efficiency of each one. Investing in mutual funds involves diversifying the portfolio by industry, geography, and asset class. Dividends are not taxable, and volatility is significantly lower. Additionally, I will focus my stock portfolio on a few stocks with long-term growth potential. The importance of staying within my sphere of competence and tracking the progress of my stock portfolio cannot be overstated. Doing your own due diligence is the only way you can gain confidence and conviction in the selection of the businesses to invest in.

If you want to increase your chances of success, you should nurture all the golden goose nests rather than pinning all your hopes on one. There is no straight line in the stock market, so you should learn to embrace volatility. During such times, it is imperative that you take the necessary steps to protect your finances. You can accomplish this by diversifying your investments, keeping an emergency fund, and avoiding leverage, for example. When in doubt, it is always a good idea to seek professional financial advice. Ultimately, the goal is to nurture multiple golden goose nests in order to create consistent growth, even if each nest produces only one golden egg, regardless of market conditions.

Bonus tip: Always plan your exit strategy before entering any new investments to optimise your investment portfolio. You can find more information on my investing strategy at https://www.isabellahong.com/services.

It's great that you have made it so far in reading this book. Your mastery of personal wealth management has reached the third and final stage!

Chapters 1-3 have focused on your psychology, allowing you to open your mind and see beyond your current perceptions of yourself and what you can accomplish. A Wealth Blueprint is presented in Chapters 4 and 5 so that you can effectively manage your money. In Chapters 6-10, I outline my method for creating an infinite income loop based on the thought process behind my investing strategy. My final chapter will outline my eleven-year wealth optimisation journey to help you gain a better understanding of how I achieved financial freedom before the age of 30.

CHAPTER 11

All Together Now

People have been asking what my secret is to achieving financial freedom. I wish I could tell them, but there's never been a secret to success. I just model myself after successful people and improvise

You're still reading? That's great!

It is impressive how dedicated you are to achieving financial success.

This chapter will provide you with a few short and actionable lessons on how to increase your wealth in this new era.

I have discussed in this book how money blueprints and mindful investing can help you achieve financial independence and maximise your wealth. Life, however, is a strategy game in itself.

To begin, I would like to tell you a personal story where we will all learn something valuable about the pitfalls of receiving unsolicited advice.

As you are aware, I was a nurse. My training encompassed both renal nursing and community nursing. In most of my cases, my patients were patients with end-stage renal failure who were dependent on dialysis in order to survive. They were required to adhere to strict dialysis routines as well as daily dietary and fluid restrictions.

Diabetes and hypertension are the most common causes of end-stage renal failure, which is further complicated by fluid overload, heart disease, and hypokalemia. Patients with this condition are usually prescribed a special diet that is low in salt, sugar, potassium, and phosphate. Any patient would have complained that the diet was quite bland and plain. Furthermore, they are usually prescribed an allowance of 800 ml to 1 litre of fluid daily.

In medicine, we know that obstinate behaviour can kill.

Despite this, in my many years of experience, I have observed that these patients do not adhere to their recommended fluid and dietary restrictions.

Patients who are not adhering to medical treatment are usually counselled, educated, and nagged by their healthcare professionals. At my hospital, I even visited their homes in order to ensure that they had the necessary tools to measure their fluid intake and to understand how they eat. Since it is fundamental to good health, I assumed that they wished to improve their health but were unaware of how to do so.

My research even delved into why haemodialysis patients failed to follow dietary and fluid restriction recommendations. I have found that haemodialysis patients endure constant suffering due to the restrictions imposed on them. Their quality of life was severely affected by the imposed restrictions.

Who is responsible for determining what is best for these patients? It is certain that we, as healthcare professionals, are well qualified to provide advice regarding best practices. Is this, however, what patients desire? Do we have the authority to make decisions regarding the quality of life of individuals on their behalf?

Is there anything similar to healthcare advice? Financial advice!

Having the knowledge and certification to provide financial advice is my forte. I am a financial consultant by profession. Having achieved financial independence, I can advise you as to what is the best course of action for you. Is that really what is best for you? No, since I know nothing about you!

I don't know what your problems are. I don't know what your situation is. I don't know what your goals are. Who am I to advise you on the prudent use of your money when I don't even know your name?

Yes, there are universal truths about money. Money does not fall from the sky. Initially, we work hard for our money, then let that money work hard for us. Every generation builds upon the foundation laid by the previous one. Why do people come to different conclusions regarding how these truths will be applied? For a variety of reasons, ideals are not always the reality.

In nursing school, my professors taught us four principles: autonomy, beneficence, justice, and nonmaleficence. Our role as nurses is to advocate for patients, but we must strike a balance between providing care and advocating for them. Despite what we know, every patient has the right to make decisions based on their values and beliefs. The same standards should be applied to financial services.

Another personal story illustrating the importance of going back to basics is presented here.

As Warren Buffett has two rules to investing:

Rule #1: Never lose money; Rule #2: Never forget Rule #1.

I have my own two rules as well:

Rule #1: Make money; Rule #2: Make more money.

I am an aggressive investor in the stock market, and I adhere to the theory of an optimally balanced portfolio in order to manage my risks. I don't like to lose money, and my focus is on (1) income generation and (2) long-term growth.

Dividends flowed into my account month after month. Prices of shares fluctuated from one day to the next, but they tended to rise from one year to the next. As a futurist, I am more concerned with creating stability in an uncertain future.

Even though Warren Buffett's investing approach is reassuring, it lacks a bit of action. After greed set in, I began to believe I could precisely spot market trends and start swing trading and day trading. In trading, I saw more volatility that played with my emotions. I have made profits on some trades, and I have lost money on others. Overall, it was a net gain, but a lot of time, energy and emotions were spent in the process. I figured it wasn't worth it, and I reverted to basics again.

In spite of the fact that digitalisation was already underway before COVID-19 hit, the pandemic has sped up innovation and increased adoption. Online gaming in Web 3.0 blew up in 2020, where people staked cryptocurrency for higher returns at "lower risks". It was a booming industry with rave reviews.

I'm no fool, I know there are no free lunches in the world of business. Players are required to deposit physical funds to stake, and their daily returns are paid in digital currency. The player could easily receive a daily return of 10%, with a potential break-even on the 27th day. This gaming business model does not make any sense, and I knew this scheme would not last. I was sceptical when I heard about it and hesitated to join the craze.

Some of my friends have, however, taken the leap of faith. Their results have been astonishing. There were no issues with the withdrawal of funds either.

Following a few weeks of observation, I fell in line, thinking I could get out before the hosts pulled the plug. And guess what? I was right!

I invested conservatively, earned an estimated 10% daily, and made periodic withdrawals. That's where I made my mistake – a costly one. Several days before I broke even, I put in a larger sum of money, and the game ended. The loss was huge.

I made this mistake out of greed and a fear of missing out.

I can't blame my friends for fraud or malice – they're just sharing an irresistible deal.

It is important to note, however, that this is not the way personal wealth optimisation is accomplished.

To achieve wealth, you must understand that it is a long-term concept accumulating over time. You will simply lose your money if it comes too easily. We are flawed in our behaviour; we can only appreciate things when they are difficult to attain.

Have you heard that 70% of wealth is lost to the second generation and 90% to the third generation? As our predecessors planted seeds to provide shade for younger generations, the traces of their hard work gradually faded away over time. Particularly in Asian cultures,

Asians are less inclined to discuss money with their children because they are concerned that their children may develop a sense of entitlement and laziness. I would say that young adults today believe they understand the value of money because they are highly educated. In reality, many individuals have difficulties managing their finances.

There is no question that some people succeed in their endeavours while others fail for various reasons. It does not matter how often you patch the cracks in a house; if the foundations are not strong, the entire house will collapse over time. **There is no secret to my success other than being consistently diligent.** From now on, this will be your secret formula as well.

In light of that caveat, let's consider some essential tips to help you make smarter financial decisions.

Financial Mastery at A Glance

The practice of introspection can provide you with a deeper understanding of who you are, your values, and the reasons for your behaviour. Make a list of all the things you thought were true and ask yourself, “Who said that? ” Often, the answer is right there in the mirror. As you may not know, we are our greatest obstacle to success.

In order to master the financial game, you must first master your self-awareness.

> *Know yourself and you will win all battles*
> – Sun Tzu

A person who does not dream of anything is unlikely to achieve anything at the end of the day. Any successful innovation begins with a clear vision of what is desired. You can stay on track by identifying achievable milestones that can serve as a guide to your growth. Based on objective measures, you will be able to determine where you are lacking and where you can improve.

Find your **WHY**, and you will find your way. Every memorable road trip requires you to step outside your comfort zone. Every good surf requires timely execution. Every standing ovation performance entails hours of dedication. It will never be an easy task. When you have identified your life's purpose, it becomes clear what matters most to you. Make sure you keep your focus, commit to your goals, and strategise decisions in alignment with them.

Staying focused on an ultimate goal is the second step in mastering the financial game.

Clarity affords focus
– Thomas Leonard

Dream it, strategise it, and make it happen! Be humble when things are going well, and compassionate when things are not going well. Failing is inevitable, but take each failure as an opportunity to learn. When you are committed to doing better next time, nothing is ever as good or bad as it seems.

Reflect on things you can't control but focus on things you can. We live in a large, complex world where risk and chance are both present. The gap between now and what you need to happen in the future is endurance, and grit makes compounding magic happen. Follow in the footsteps of your role model and make your mark.

The third step in mastering the financial game is being willing to take calculated risks.

Think like a queen. A queen is not afraid to fail. Failure is another stepping stone to greatness
– Oprah Winfrey

Those who don't know how to manage their money will be managed by their money. Having a spending plan is an essential part of our daily lives. By doing so, you will be able to clearly see what your money was spent on rather than wondering where it went. You should keep a close eye on your spending in order to ensure that you are on track for the future. You should develop a financial blueprint that will give you and your family peace of mind while working effectively towards attaining your financial and lifestyle goals.

Self-discipline is a fourth step in mastering the financial game.

> *Being rich is hard. Staying poor is hard.*
> *Choose your hard.*
> – Eric Worre

Get your priorities straight by reducing your ego so you can achieve more wealth. A key component of building wealth is sacrificing short-term desires and investing for the long term. No matter how much money you earn, building wealth will not be possible if you have financial leaks. You can achieve this by practising delayed gratification.

In reality, nobody is as impressed with your possessions as you are. It might seem that you desire a luxury home or branded bag, but what you really crave is respect and admiration. A kind and humble heart is more likely to bring you those things than acting posh and blingy.

A fifth step in mastering the financial game is planning and investing for the future.

> *I don't believe in spending money lavishly, now that I'm making money.*
>
> – Ansel Elgort

Money is not yours to pursue. It's yours to master. Learn how to use money to earn multiple sources of passive income to spend more time with the people and things that are most important to you. The ability to control your time can be one of the most powerful and universal contributors to happiness. The most important aspect of freedom is the ability to do what you want, when you want, with whom you want, and for as long as you want.

Earn first! The first priority should be to earn money and establish a healthy cash flow. This will allow you to maximise the potential of your portfolio to ensure long-term financial success. Paying your bills on time is an important part of your financial well-being. It's also important to earn more than you spend to keep your cash flow positive.

Protect your assets for peace of mind. Take care of your money, so you don't have to worry. There are two factors that can affect your income: health and retrenchment. While you are able to influence the length of your unemployment period, you are not able to control how long you need to spend regaining your health. The importance of wealth protection differs from individual to individual. Nevertheless, the underlying question is, "Will it give me peace of mind?" This is the best universal guidepost for all financial decisions.

Save. Just save! Oftentimes, people save to achieve a particular goal, such as buying a home, acquiring a vehicle, or taking a vacation. Apart from material comfort, one good reason to save is to prepare for things that are difficult to predict or define. All roads to success are paved with surprises. A free cash flow is a hedge against life's inevitable ability to surprise you at the most unfortunate time.

Invest in constructing your own infinity income loop. The most powerful way to improve your investment results is to extend your time horizon. Investing is a game of patience. With compounding, small investments become larger, and large errors become insignificant. There is no way to neutralise luck and risk, but it can help align people's results with what they deserve.

It is always advisable to invest in yourself first. Your knowledge will give you the confidence and conviction you need to implement your strategy. Ideally, your financial portfolio should be sufficiently diversified to minimise risk while maximising your wealth. It is true that a bull market makes everyone appear smart, but a bear market reveals the truth. Feeling lost or confused? Refer back to the fundamentals! Don't let your emotions cloud your judgement.

Mastering your emotional intelligence is the sixth step in the journey toward financial mastery.

> *Financial security and independence are like a three-legged stool resting on saving, insurance and investments.*
>
> – Brian Tracy

Life is a journey with different chapters, each with its own challenges and priorities. Even among the smartest and most knowledgeable individuals, the issue of personal wealth optimisation can be contentious since everyone has different goals and priorities. You can be sure that there will be a lot of mess.

The key is to develop a strategy that works for you and to remain open-minded throughout the process. Greater responsibilities come with greater stress, and as we age, our needs and wants naturally change. Depending on the extreme nature of your past decisions, you may regret them more as you age. You need to determine how you wish to live your life and not be influenced by others who are playing a different game.

Money is only one tool for achieving wealth. Among the true riches are freedom of time, good health, happiness, and spiritual well-being. To make money work for you in the long run, you must use it wisely. A poor financial decision can result in a lifetime of regrets, while a good financial decision can bring abundance. Success is determined by the value you provide to others. You should strive to make this world a better place than it was when you first found it by adding value to it. In due course, money will follow.

Authenticity is the final step to achieving financial mastery.

> *Success isn't about how much money you make. It's about the difference you make in people's lives.*
> – Michelle Obama

The concept of personal finance is a crucial component of everyone's life, and mastering it involves mastering oneself. Playing the financial game effectively can lead to financial freedom, whereas failing to do so will result in working forever for money. A person's financial decisions have an impact on more than just their personal finances and can be seen in other aspects of their lives as well. As T. Harv Eker famously said, "What you do is how you do everything."

In these pages, I hope you have found something of value and some comfort. This journey has come to an end, and I would like to extend an invitation to you. It would be a pleasure to hear how this book has impacted you and continue the conversation. Please feel free to contact me through my website or social media.

Website: http://www.isabellahong.com

Telegram: https://t.me/FINANCIALmissyInvests

Let's continue to explore these ideas and develop our understanding of ourselves and the world as a whole. Your financial success is something I look forward to.

Acknowledgements

My heartfelt thanks go to the following individuals who generously lent their support during the creation of this book. Their contributions were invaluable and made all the difference in bringing my vision to life. Thank you for being there for me every step of the way.

To Anna Von Zinner, my mentor and editor, thank you for your unwavering support and guidance. Your firm hand helped steer me back on track when I lost focus, and your endless enthusiasm and patience gave me the confidence to complete this book. I am deeply grateful for your faith in me and your belief in my abilities. Thank you for being an exceptional mentor, editor and coach.

To my dear father and mother, I extend my sincerest gratitude for the love and guidance you have given me throughout my upbringing. Your method of tough love and strict training has shaped me into the strong and independent woman I am today. I am forever grateful for the challenges you presented, which have aided my growth and fortitude.

Without your guidance, I might have fallen into complacency and entitlement. I am proud to say that my financial independence by 30 resulted from your unwavering support and daily guidance. I am blessed to have such wonderful parents like you both.

To the Next Level team, I extend my heartfelt thanks for the numerous opportunities provided to me to strengthen my knowledge in investing and entrepreneurship. I am honoured to have had the chance to speak alongside well-known names such as Mary Buffett and Nicole Buffett. Your guidance and support have been instrumental in my growth and development, both in my mindset and ability to overcome obstacles. I am truly grateful for your contributions to my success.

References

Chapter 1

Griffith, E. (2014). *Why startups fail, according to their founders*. Retrieved from https://fortune.com/2014/09/25/why-startups-fail-according-to-their-founders/

Skynova. *The Entrepreneurial Journey*. Retrieved from https://www.skynova.com/blog/the-entrepreneurial-journey

Wai, J., & Rindermann, H. (2017). What goes into high educational and occupational achievement? Education, brains, hard work, networks, and other factors. *High Ability Studies, 28*(1), 127-145. doi:10.1080/13598139.2017.1302874

Chapter 2

Graziosi, D. 2019. *Millionaire Success Habits: The Gateway to Wealth & Prosperity,* United States, Hay House Inc.

Hamilton, R. n.d. Profile Report. *Wealth Dynamics.*

Chapter 3

Alund, N. N. (2022, 20 June 2022). *How much does lunch with Warren Buffett cost? Just $19 million*. Retrieved from https://www.usatoday.com/story/money/2022/06/20/warren-buffett-ebay-auction-lunch/7681611001/

Chapter 5

HOUSEL, M. 2020. The Psychology of Money: Timeless lessons on wealth, greed, and happiness, UK, Harriman House.

Park, S. Q., Kahnt, T., Dogan, A., Strang, S., Fehr, E., & Tobler, P. N. (2017). A neural link between generosity and happiness. *Nat Commun, 8*, 15964. doi:10.1038/ncomms15964

Slickdeals. (2019). *Americans Feel Guilty Spending an Average $277,680 in Their Adult Life Time, According to New Survey Findings Revealed by Slickdeals.* Retrieved from https://www.prnewswire.com/news-releases/americans-feel-guilty-spending-an-average-277-680-in-their-adult-life-time-according-to-new-survey-findings-revealed-by-slickdeals-300841669.html

Chapter 6

Kiyosaki, R.T. (2012). *Cashflow Quadrant: Guide to Financial Freedom*, US, Plata Publishing, LLC.

Chapter 8

Robbins, T. 2017. *Unshakeable*, US, Simon & Schuster Paperbacks.

About the Author

Isabella is quickly making a name for herself in the finance world. With her focus on personal finance, she has been honoured to share her insights and knowledge with audiences alongside renowned figures such as Mary Buffett, Nicole Buffett, Sean Seah, and Sam Cawthorn. Her thought-provoking ideas and perspectives have established her as a key influencer in the finance industry.

Isabella's commitment to personal finance shines through in her engaging and educational presentations, which have made her a go-to source of practical, empowering advice for millennials. Her unique approach has earned her a reputation as a mentor and finance specialist who truly cares about helping others succeed.

Based in Singapore, when she's not inspiring others in the finance world, Isabella can be found indulging in her love of surfing and exploring the waves across Asia.

Connect with Isabella:

Made in the USA
Las Vegas, NV
28 April 2023

71226199R00114